# Professional Roles in Society and Government: The English Case

**ERWIN C. HARGROVE**
*Brown University*

104897

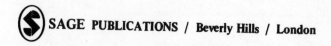
SAGE PUBLICATIONS / Beverly Hills / London

*For information address:*

**SAGE** PUBLICATIONS, INC.
275 South Beverly Drive
Beverly Hills, California 90212

**SAGE** PUBLICATIONS LTD
St George's House / 44 Hatton Garden
London E C 1

International Standard Book Number 0-8039-0189-5

Library of Congress Catalog Card No. 72-89164

FIRST PRINTING

# CONTENTS

# CONTENTS

# LIST OF TABLES

# Professional Roles in Society and Government: The English Case

## CHAPTER I
## THE ENGLISH SYNTHESIS OF TRADITION AND MODERNITY

**England was the first modern society** in the Western world, but it has never become a wholly modern society. Many traditional, preindustrial values thrive. The development of experimental science, of technology applied to industrial development, and of the folkways and institutions of modern capitalism were all accomplished against a historical background of values and institutions which were not fully challenged or demolished. Rather, those very traditional institutions provided the national unity which facilitated the transition to modernity. A strong monarchy, a constitutional settlement, and a sense of national separateness and community had been developed before the advent of the industrial way of life (Rothman, 1961).

A subculture of an aristocratic governing class was the chief agent of traditional values. Eighteenth-century England was a society in which

AUTHOR'S NOTE: *Some of the ideas and data in this paper have been presented in shorter form in "Values and Change: A Comparison of Young Elites in England and America,"* Political Studies *XVII, September 1969, and in "Tradition and Change in England, Innovators in the Professions and the Polity,"* Comparative Politics, *July 1972. I should like to thank Richard Rose and Dennis Kavanaugh for their helpful comments on an earlier draft of this paper.*

separate estates were bound together through traditionally defined duties, rights, and attitudes. The governing class felt a responsibility for the general welfare of all classes and in this sense continued many of the values of the Tudor monarchy, which had been the initial basis of the strong sense of national community.

The premises of nineteenth-century liberalism and of the philosophic radicals stood in sharp contrast to the ideals of the society which was to be transformed. A pyramidal, paternalist model of society was challenged by an atomistic, individualistic model. The Benthamite revolution of the mid-nineteenth century was an effort to rationalize all traditional institutions in terms of the new values.

However, the actual result was a synthesis of traditional and modern values in the dominant institutions of the society and in elite strata which faced both directions and fused both kinds of values in their own lives. This synthesis was a result of the strong sense of national community which softened the sharp edges of the contending traditions. The historic, aristocratic governing class coopted the industrial middle classes into the traditional institutions and themselves, in turn, adapted and adjusted to the new society. Ascription and achievement were combined in the character of the great public schools, the reformed civil service, the ancient universities, and the parliamentary political parties, as well as in business and the professions. The final fruit was a cluster of Victorian elites and institutions which were laced through with both traditional and modern themes. The values of capitalism were not fully triumphant because they had been softened by traditional Tory notions about the importance of national community, by the aristocratic ideal of the gentleman, and belief in the importance of service to the state. A new governing class emerged which was neither fully traditional nor wholly modern, but a uniquely English blend of both elements.

The same cycle of challenge, reform, and synthesis has been repeated in the twentieth century, with socialism as the protagonist against both traditional Tory and liberal capitalist cultures. Yet, in their very challenge, radicals and socialists combined elements of Toryism and liberalism. They appealed to a Tory past against liberalism, a memory of what had come before, of a genuine national community. And they built on the radical strain of liberalism in their desire for social equality (Rothman, 1961). However, as in the synthesis of Tory and liberal, the twentieth-century radical was also coopted into the established institutions at the same time as radicalism helped to transform those institutions. English socialism has been reformist rather than revolutionary. And the modern welfare state contains strands of Tory noblesse oblige, liberal reform, and socialist ideals of equality.

The society is still not wholly modern in the sense that mores and institutions have not been fully rationalized to serve the gods of modernity—maximum productivity and efficiency. Many preindustrial values survive (Rose, 1965). A high degree of ascription and elitism exists in the class structure and is particularly manifested in education. There is an uneven commitment to entrepreneurial values among the business and industrial elites. And there still seems to be a widespread belief in the importance of the amateur and generalist in the governance of the society as opposed to the expert. One could very well argue that a high price has been paid for the high degree of national community and the method of innovation through cooptation. The price is that root-and-branch social reform and genuine radical social transformation have not been possible. The forces which have permitted reform have also prevented radical change.

However, this characterization is too static because a new Benthamite revolution is under way. One can identify three phases of this change since the early sixties: first, a period of scathing social criticism and satire (Sampson, 1962), then a period of development of new ideologies for social and political change, and, finally, the introduction and implementation of reform (Crick, 1967). This revolution is challenging all those values and norms in both the traditionalist Tory and the socialist subcultures, which are seen as obstacles to the rationalization of society in terms of efficiency and productivity. Two complementary themes seem to be at work: first, the need to develop better problem-solving capabilities in the society; second, the need for wider participation in community decision-making and for the wider fulfillment of the social aspirations of all citizens.

Much of the literature of dissatisfaction focused upon the leadership of the society. The Fulton report in 1968 on the higher civil service condemned the "amateurism" of civil servant mandarins. Political scientists and journalists attacked the inability of Parliament, an assembly of part-time politicians, to control the executive in any effective way (Crick, 1965). Genteel, inefficient managerial styles were said to be at the root of slow economic growth (Caves et al., 1968).

The critics scattered their shots, but two main themes were criticisms of elite political culture and the chief institutions of national government. Elite political culture was depicted as too much addicted to the styles of the generalist amateur and too fond of incrementalist solutions. Root-and-branch solutions were avoided if at all possible, and yet Britain was seen to be floundering in a wave of uncertainty about her role in the world. The institutions of government were depicted as too hierarchical and too closed with the result, it is alleged, that policy was not sufficiently scrutinized and debated before it carried and then proved to be disastrous. Critics called for opening institutions to greater publicity and infusions of outside expertise in order to improve the quality of policy. An American political scientist, Kenneth Waltz (1967), studying British government in the late fifties and early sixties, developed such criticisms from an American perspective and thereby anticipated a subsequent stream of English criticisms of their own institutions from the same point of view. The wave of domestic criticism was rooted in what were taken to be evident policy failures during that period: the vacillation about entering Europe and the eventual temporary failure to do so, the stagnant economy, and the failure of nerve of a theretofore self-confident Tory governing elite.

However, by the mid-sixties, all major parties had taken over modernization as a strong theme, and a number of institutional innovations took place in line with these social criticisms and the theme of modernization:

(1) Several new universities were founded, most of which gave special place to the social sciences.

(2) Technical institutes were advanced to university status.

(3) Two graduate schools of business management, based upon American models, were founded.

(4) Scientific and technological planning for national needs was begun by central government.

(5) National economic planning was introduced successively by Conservative and Labour governments.

(6) Government-sponsored experiments in institutional reform were initiated: (a) The Fulton Royal Commission on the civil service called for wholesale renovation of the home civil service to afford less secrecy, give generalist administrators better training and competence in social science, give professionals in the specialist grades full equality with generalist administrators, provide for more lateral entry from outside into the civil service for temporary periods and for in-service training to teach civil servants to be organizational managers as well as advisers to ministers. (b) Specialized committees of the House of Commons were created in a deliberate effort to temper the grain of Cabinet government by requiring ministers and civil servants to discuss proposals and submit information to such committees in order that the ideas of government might be scrutinized and their administrative practices

ventilated. The key assumption behind this innovation was the belief that more open government would produce better policy (Mackintosh, 1971). (c) The Redcliffe-Maud Commission on local government recommended a wholesale reorganization and rationalization of local government (Royal Commission on Local Government in England, 1969).

In each of these cases, significant steps toward implementation of the recommendations have been taken by Labour and Conservative governments. The full working out of the ideas will take many years. One could characterize all these changes and many others as a modern-day Benthamite revolution which will alter the structure and appearance of old institutions and infuse them with new roles and a new utilitarian spirit in order to make them more adaptable and functional for the needs of modern Britain.

The English have shown great ability to put new wine in old bottles, to graft the new onto the old in new combinations. And this is a much-required virtue in modern society. The study of social change in contemporary Britain is therefore likely to be of value for an understanding of constructive methods of change and innovation.

## YOUNG PROFESSIONALS

This is a study of the ideas of specific agents of change and innovation, young professional men who are trying to innovate within their fields and in government in terms of the dominant English social mood. Our purpose is to discover through their own words and eyes their picture of changing English society and their role in helping to change it.

We often think of the professions as conservative forces bent on protecting their corporate autonomy against external interference or regulation, whether from clients or government. They can become vested interests which refuse to develop new forms of service to clients and society. The professional ethic of autonomy, like the bureaucratic rule, becomes an end in itself, rather than a means. However, we could also envision professionals as innovators within their fields and within institutions. Institutions need new knowledge to solve new problems. The professions are the carriers of applied knowledge. They are brokers between the ivory tower of discovery of knowledge and the world of power (Price, 1965). Professionals are often therefore called upon to contribute to increasing the capabilities of institutions toward solving the problems of society.

Also, because they are to a large extent cross-national fraternities, the professions can be active conduits for cross-national learning and borrowing of ideas and techniques. More or less universal ideas can be transplanted and adapted to national settings through the efforts of professionals to better serve their clients or the institutions, including government, within which they work.

Professions are also embedded in the norms and values of a national culture and help to carry and implement the values of that culture. Therefore, insofar as they seek to introduce new knowledge and new practices into the institutions of society, innovative professionals are agents of culture change and agents for the adaptation of the social system to new tasks.

For these reasons, the study of social change in England could properly focus on professionals as agents of innovation. The implicit ethic of the innovative professional, as hypothesized above, would seem to be very congruent with the Benthamite spirit abroad in England.

This is thus a study of the ideologies of young professionals, who are innovators in their fields and in social and political institutions in England today. The purpose of the study is to build on their ideas about innovation and change in England to develop a number of hypotheses about:

(1) patterns of innovation in England;
(2) the role of professionals in innovation in society and polity;
(3) the role of professionals in cross-cultural borrowing;
(4) the congruence of professional values and norms with social and political ideology in times of change.

## METHODOLOGY

A reputational method was used for the selection of subjects. Groups of informants in the several professions to be studied or experts on those professions were asked to identify especially "innovative" professional men in their thirties or early forties. The criteria of "innovative" were:

(1) people who were pioneering in the new role of temporary "in and outer" in British government as advisers to ministers and civil servants;
(2) redefiners of professional norms and roles for a profession;
(3) people with original ideas about public policy which they were pursing through their profession.

The subjects did not have to possess all three of these characteristics to be named or selected. Given the kind of person I wanted to study, the reputational method of selection seemed best. A statistical sampling of professional directories or government positions would not have achieved the same result. The study was necessarily confined to a small group of respondents, and I wished to study individuals who were playing important innovative roles in the society at that point in time.

In order to ensure that the biases of my informants did not unduly shape the selection of respondents, I met with each informant to discuss the criteria in light of the changes taking place in each profession and in English society. The informants were themselves selected on the basis of my knowledge of English life and people. I picked those persons whom I thought best situated to identify innovative young professionals.

The informants are described in Appendix A and the subjects in Appendix B. I never relied upon one informant for all the subjects chosen, although there was overlap between the names given me in almost every case. Most of the people whose names were given me were written and asked to take part in a study of the beliefs of young professionals. Only a handful declined. The interviews were conducted from January to June 1968, in London and other English cities. They were recorded on tape and transcribed. Each interview was two hours long.

The questionnaire was a checklist of topics rather than an insistent structure, and the questions were deliberately open-ended. The subjects were encouraged to develop whatever themes they wished from the original starting point, although a basic outline was maintained. Each group of questions was intended to explore the thinking of the subject about English society in the past, present, and future. What goals were they working for and why? What changes did they see as needed and why? What common beliefs would appear in their thinking about these different spheres? What descriptions of innovation and of their own roles in change would they give, and how might these be linked to their general appraisal of society?

This was frankly an exploratory study into the thinking of professionals, not a case study of innovators in action. The latter seemed premature at the time. The purpose was to develop propositions for subsequent research, not to test them. This study should now be followed by a much more extensive survey of elite opinion and complementary intensive case studies of particular cases of institutional innovation.

## CHAPTER II
## ENGLISH SOCIETY AND INSTITUTIONS:
## THE PATTERN OF CHANGE

### NATIONALITY AND VALUES

A person's consciousness of himself as a citizen of a particular national society is shaped by his understanding of what that society is. Sense of self and sense of nationality are intertwined. Western man has had a sense of history as having a beginning, an end, and a purpose. The idea of national mission and purpose emerged out of that view of history. Every society has its own version of how it came to be, where it is going, and what its dominant values are and should be.

The desire to modernize is thus both a rejection of some aspects of tradition and an affirmation of others. The essential purposes of the society, the nation, must be reaffirmed. This creates a dilemma of how much of the past to save and what to jettison.

This dilemma is both collective and individual. Individuals feel strong pulls within themselves toward both tradition and change, toward old and new values and old and new symbols. This emerges clearly when these Englishmen were asked what they most admired about Britain.

The question was designed to tap the degree to which they looked to their country, its culture and institutions, as sources of their own social and political values.

The answers were striking in their similarity:

(1) Tolerance, moderation, capacity for compromise—24
(2) Decency, civility—8
(3) Stable society—4
(4) Free democratic institutions—3
(5) History—3
(6) Mixed—4

The word tolerance was cited more often than any other single word, and it was used in a general context of respect for moderation, balance, and stability. Here are illustrative comments, the first from a political scientist; the second, a lawyer:

I think the best thing about it is still a sort of gentleness and innocence in the relationships of most people really to strangers, to people other than the ones they're under an obligation to. There's a kind of naivete which is very attractive, I think, in English public life. Not necessarily, not an intraelite naivete, although there are elements of it even there, but there's a lack of hardness and there's a sort of softness that's partly, it's all bound up with deference and all those things. But there's also a quality of a lack of ambition and so on which is a very attractive thing, I think ... people aren't so fierce with each other and so aggressive and so intolerant as they are, for example, in Italy or France or certainly not in the United States. I mean it's part of the fact that we're a very incomplete industrial modern country—there's the sort of important hangovers from a more leisurely time.

I would say it was a sort of combination of tolerance on the one hand and a capacity to do things in an orderly, quiet, moderate way. An ability to evolve without serious massive disagreements. Somehow or other managing to share a tremendous superstructural infrastructure of beliefs which somehow lead to a civilized existence.

The answers citing democratic institutions mentioned the rule of law, opportunities for widespread participation in government and the absence of dictators. Those who spoke in historical terms praised the transition from Empire to Commonwealth, the development of the industrial revolution, and the political history of Britain.

The mixed answers were combinations of these themes: fairness, lack of turmoil, tolerance, honesty, stability, rule of law, liberty. All in all, we find a rather impressive agreement on the qualities of the society to be valued.

The question next posed was: "Of what are you most critical about this country?"

(1) Resistance to change—21
(2) Social inequality—10
(3) Conduct of government—7
(4) Inefficiency—4
(5) Mixed—4

The chief criticism was the social conservatism which permitted Englishmen to be tradition-bound, complacent, and without initiative to innovate. A picture is given of people who are entirely too comfortable. Here are some comments, the first from a barrister and Conservative Parliamentary candidate; the second, an economist:

The immense sluggishness and resistance to economic change, immense protectionism, defensiveness in all social and economic groups.

I think there is a great deal of uncriticalness about institutions which one resents. The Bodleian Library isn't the greatest thing in the world. Oxford University techniques of teaching aren't necessarily the best for all sorts of undergraduates. There's a lot of that which I find very annoying and worst of all, it gradually sucks one in oneself; one finds one can't all the time be criticizing and questioning and dissenting, one has to go along with it some of the time and one can just hope that it'll evolve.

Criticisms of social inequality ranged from unhappiness with the entire class structure to concern about particular manifestations of it, but the general theme was clear. The cards of British life are loaded in favor of some people and against others. Here is a barrister, a Labour Parliamentary candidate:

> I'm most critical about our failure to develop proper educational facilities for a large proportion of the population. I'm pretty critical about our acceptance of an income structure which still has a large number of working men with families on incomes . . . of less than sixteen or seventeen pounds a week.

Another theme was the indecisiveness of government, its inability to act to solve problems. The complaints were more a mood than an analysis. The same is true of comments about general social inefficiency. A business manager, also a Tory Parliamentary candidate, felt that the British "humanist" attitude to the solving of problems led to a preference for solutions which did not come from the logical applications of science. The debit of this was:

> we do not pursue lines consistently. We are much too likely to go after new things. We don't develop things. We get deflected. For example, in the economy we are trying to avoid problems and dodge work. This is the debit side of the humanist attitude to problems. We don't worship capitalist gods and money as in the United States.

His point was that the British were technologically innovative but had little interest in the organizational follow-through to develop ideas. Their innovativeness was a form of technological "amateurism."

The mixed responses were combinations of criticisms mentioned by the others, the most frequent combinations being criticism of resistance to change and class prejudice and inequality.

Clearly a dominant theme is that national virtues and vices are intertangled in many ways. Many answers explicitly recognized that the qualities admired and those criticized seemed to be two sides of the same coin. Here is an economist, a former civil servant, with strong Labour party ties, beginning to say what he most admires and turning the coin over:

> I think of the British people—their habits of mind ... in some ways what often looks like their inertness, laziness, insularity and so on. It does seem to me to add up to a sort of discretion, stability, maturity. ... There's a sort of all round amateurism, muddleheadedness, muddling through, softness, rounding of the edges about people in this country which I think—although you miss a lot of the tricks a lot of the time—it's a comforting fact.

An executive and Liberal Party Parliamentary candidate:

> The thing I most admire about this country is tolerance ... and within that a tradition of decency and kindliness ... at the same time they are the things which produce a certain slowness and conservatism and resistance to change which the bastards of this world don't have. So once again, if you don't want to see this country submerged beneath a wave of bad debts, you have to show how far the old-fashioned virtues can be reconciled with the aggressiveness and competitiveness and the other qualities that one believes to be necessary for an industrial society. ... I think the virtues and vices are inextricably mixed up.

Twenty-two people explicitly said that they saw two sides of the coin in the sense that national virtues and vices were entangled. All of them gave answers of admiring tolerance and stability but fearing that these very virtues also involved conservatism and resistance to change. Several mentioned that it might be difficult to separate vices from virtues, and a few wondered if too high a price might have to be paid in losing attractive qualities by an attack on conservatism and resistance to change. However, almost all of them were keen to try and had hopes that the good qualities of tolerance and stability could be kept in a more innovative tempo. As one manager said in regard to the dilemma of keeping British "humanism" and yet having a more dynamic society: "if we have a role in the world, it is to have it both ways."

Seven presented the same theme in their answers but did not explicitly mention a two-sides-to-the-coin problem. Two put forward the same theme but denied any linkage between positive and negative traits.

The remaining fifteen made no connection between admired and criticized traits and presented no obvious connection of theme. Ten of these were critical of an inequalitarian class structure. There may be a connection between such a social structure and certain habits of tolerance and stability, but they did not advance such an idea.

We will be following the theme of innovation throughout this study, and the dominant tone has already been set. They greatly admire the stability, tolerance, and capacity for gradual reform of their society. But they want much more rapid and radical innovation than is occurring. The very things of which they are critical lead us into the need for reform: tolerance of old institutions and habits, whether they work or not; lack of dynamism and drive, particularly in economic pursuits; social inequality and class snobbery; amateurism in leaders. In short, Britain is not seen as a sufficiently "modern" society. One can see an implicit model of change in the comments of some few of these people that can be put forward as a hypothesis at this point.

This model follows from a perception of good and bad traits as entangled. This presents the innovator with the problem of how to innovate and yet avoid throwing out the baby with the bath water. The solution is to find a new balance between tradition and change which preserves the best of the old with the desired features of the new.

So we will see a strong "Benthamite" strain in the thinking of these people, a drive for "modernization" in terms of the qualities needed in leaders and in the structure and organization of institutions. However, the method of innovation will be the historic incremental one of piling new additions onto old layers of habits and institutions. Here is a city planner who was quite critical of the "amateurism" of British governmental leaders, particularly high civil servants:

One of the remarkable things—it's almost paradoxical—if you take one level of this society, it's full of inertia: trade unions, the civil service, in business. And yet, if you take different cuts through the thing, you can find equally persuasive reasons for leading you to believe an enormous amount of subtle change is going on at the same time.

Some things can be held stable . . . and yet other things can take on quite dynamic change. That is happening. It leads to a selectivity of view. If you want to see pigheaded resistance to change, you've got loads of examples. On the other hand, you can find all sorts of evidence of quite drastic changes taking place. If we wait for the Fulton Committee's report on the civil service, here again might be capacity to bring about quite fundamental change and yet keep some outer shells looking very much the same.

This is the implicit model of innovation that, as we will see, appears in much of their thinking. One must strike a new balance between old values and habits and new goals and methods.

There is one qualification which must be made in the hypothesis that the majority of these people accept this model of change. Those who are most critical of inequalities they see in the class system are less likely to see a two-sides-of-the-coin dilemma with regard to reform in this area. With two exceptions, each of these ten people is a supporter of the Labour party. The other two are a Liberal economist and a "Tory democrat" planner, both of whom see themselves as reformers. This suggests that the method of seeking a balance between new and old may be more common with regard to institutional change and common to all except those who are critical of the social system on ideological grounds.

Other than this, there were no links between those qualities of the society which were admired or disliked and either profession or ideology. We have been exploring a diffuse set of sentiments which seem common to all these people. One can thus suggest that nationality is a source of social and political values in and of itself.

## IDEOLOGY

This is a study of the ideas about the "good society" held by a number of different people. Our definition of "ideology" is simply that notion.

The subject of ideology in the interviews was approached by asking people to put themselves on an ideological spectrum as conservatives, liberals, radicals, and the like. This first approximation at self-anchoring was then followed up by probing into what was meant by such terms, why they saw themselves in that way, and how such a self-characterization was related to their ideas about the good society, about the future, about parties and politics, social class, and specific tasks of government in the society.

These individuals have been placed in left, right, and center ideological clusters according to an assessment of their relative position on the ideological spectrum.

There are three great modern political parties in England—Conservative, Liberal, and Labour—and three broad, corresponding intellectual traditions which are far older than each party (Cristoph, 1965). Each tradition has developed across time, much as the English constitution has developed. New layers have been grafted with old in new versions of continuity and

TABLE 1
**IDEOLOGICAL SPECTRUM**

| Left | Center | Right |
|------|--------|-------|
| 18 | 19 | 9 |

change. The modern conservative tradition is thus a fusion of the Tory squirearchy, and its defense of throne and altar of the eighteenth century, the capitalist conservatism of Sir Robert Peel and the Tory democracy of Disraeli, with modern, managerial conservatism. The liberal tradition has come from the atomism of Locke and Bentham and the Utilitarians to the moral community of T. H. Green and Leonard Hobhouse, and the modern reforming party of Lloyd George and Asquith. English socialism is primarily about equality and somewhat less about collectivism, with a strong attachment to the cooperative society.

These three traditions were found here, and each seemed to be in a process of revision as they sought to adapt tradition to new problems.

The most prominent theme cited by those on the English Left was that of social equality. The same phrases recur: "a radical egalitarian temperament"—"want steady structural change, more equality, more distribution of material and nonmaterial benefits"—"don't want industrial values to extend to everything"—"taking equality seriously, eliminating socially caused privileges"—"want accountability of private wealth, want industrial democracy." However, very few of these people mentioned government ownership of private industry as the key to their ideology. This was not seen as relevant to the problem of social inequality, which was the main concern. A few comments give the flavor of these views. First, from an economist, temporarily working in Whitehall:

> I don't like the capitalist rat race and I would like to have a mixed society in which power is widely dispersed amongst the social classes and in which it might be possible to build values which are not financial ones. I think I believe in public ownership as a way of taking power out of private hands to a limited extent. I prefer universal social services and lots of things like railways and milk becoming free goods, because I think this is a nicer society. I don't like people clinking money all the time. But how one gets there and what one does is a different matter.

> Also, a certain inclination to meddle and interfere with the working of the machine, you know, the economic machine which, I suppose, is a part of socialist dogma that there is a social purpose to be served over and above that which the profit motive will automatically bring about. But there is a technical, economic argument . . . about whether what one does in one's intervention is to merely restore the solution which would be brought about by a perfectly competitive model, if there were not the imperfections, or whether one's substituting an entirely new objective function or whatever you want to call it for what one wants the machine to do. I incline myself to the second view, although I defend myself in most controversies as belonging to the first view.

In controversies within the government machine, he takes the first view and seeks to optimize capitalism, but his actual views are more radical. But, he questions "How one gets there." In fact, these "socialists" have no blueprint for the future society beyond a desire for greater equality and a less acquisitive climate.

From a lawyer, active in race relations law and politics:

I don't think I have worked out theory. I'm not a utopian. I don't have a picture of a complete ideal society somewhere ahead which I'm moving towards. I'm an ameliorist.

I don't like an acquisitive society. I don't really like a capitalist society—have to tolerate one for some time.

These people are reaching beyond capitalism for something better without being quite sure how to achieve it. Not all of those of the Left explicitly reject capitalism. But all are radical in wanting a great deal more social equality.

Those on the Right are of two kinds, the more traditional Tory who combines certain attitudes of paternalism and noblesse oblige with a capitalist value of competition and economic development, and the majority who work out of a strictly capitalist viewpoint. All share a mood of skepticism about idealism and see themselves as tough-minded realists in contrast to the idealists of the Left. Phrases recur: "take the individual as he is and don't try to change him"—"a crude philosophy about incentives and return"—"must maximize freedom of choice, release political controls"—"some people have to be bosses, socialism forgets human nature."

A barrister and Conservative candidate presented a classic case of the different strands in Conservative tradition. He accepts a stratified, hierarchical society as good if it permits mobility of the talented. However, he is seeking to graft ideas of economic "liberalism" (in the European sense of capitalist economy and limited government) onto the older Tory notions. And it is all done in terms of a commitment to ideological flexibility which is very much a Conservative style. To illustrate these points, we will range across the interview:

I think the recognition of some stratification is a source of strength to society. If it becomes a complete kaleidoscopic shakeup socially and economically in every generation, which is the kind of theoretical ultimate of the meritocracy, then people lose their bearings. ... If you haven't got any naturally placed leaders in society other than those who happen to have been economically successful starting from the same zero baseline in every generation, or those who happen to have been intellectually successful in competitive examinations, the thing is so fluid that most ordinary people who are not really in the competitive race anyway don't know quite who the hell is running them. They don't quite have a respect for the institutions of government and the pattern of society which is preserved, if you like, by the hierarchy descending from the Monarchy.

However, when he was asked what he was most critical of in Britain, his answer seemed in some ways to contradict his admiration for aristocracy:

The immense sluggishness and resistance to economic change, immense protectionism, defensiveness in all social and economic groups. The extent to which the whole of our economic and social thinking has been dominated by the pursuit of equality as a primary objective of social policy. I think it has stifled and destroyed. It is summed up in the awful phrase "it isn't fair." And if our kids ever say that something isn't fair, they are suppressed because life isn't fair. And if everyone is going around looking at every change with a view to seeing how unfair it is, then nothing ever happens.

Most of the innovation we need in the institutions of society should be designed to make them less politically and therefore sluggishly controlled, more market-controlled and therefore more capable of responding to individual competitive pressures. And egalitarianism has taken sides with conservatism to protect institutions in a way to suppress the individual urge to achieve. I think most worthwhile change comes from individual energies, bringing it about.

When asked if his desire for a more competitive society was not contrary to his admiration for ascriptive values, he answered:

No. A lot of them [aristocrats] are very adaptable. Some of them will go to the wall. But what I'm really concerned about is not that they should be protected from going. They are there now, and they are staying in a tenacious way. But that their value is not respected because the duds stay as well. I don't mind the prospect of aristocrats declining, because I suspect that most of them, because of aristocracy, would in fact survive rather well. And if they seem to be surviving in a more competitive society, then they will be that much the more respected.

When asked if there is a theory here that a society needs an elite or elites to provide standards and goals, he said, "Yes. A degree of continuity about a leadership elite which obviously can't be frozen, and it would be disastrous if it was."

He is attempting to join two different Conservative traditions, the Tory and the Whig—the Tory paternalist and Whig economic liberalism—in order to make the Conservative Party, with its ancient wisdom about the art of governance, a vehicle for loosening up the economic, social, and political structures of the society.

> The Conservative party has always declined to commit itself to a particular economic or social ideology and has therefore survived and been adaptable because of its balancing role. And I've no doubt that at the present time it needs to be leaning massively towards nineteenth-century economic liberalism.

> I wouldn't regard myself as a conservative with a small c, except in the sort of hierarchical view of society that I've tried to present. I'd regard myself as a radical in terms of institutional reform, I think. And a massive economic liberal—and I'm dominated by economic liberalism more than anything else I think. But I'm very impatient with our institutions. I just don't think they are best reformed by making them bigger and better. Want to make them smaller and more sensitive and more efficient.

He illustrates the residue of preindustrial, ascriptive stands in English conservative thought, the emphasis upon elites, community, and continuity. He accepts these values, but seeks to loosen them up with a whiff of economic liberalism and a more competitive society. Seen in this context, he is a Tory radical and a modernizer. The other people on the Right express many of the same ideas, although few pay as much deference to the ascriptive dimension as he does. They are much more likely to talk about the need for a more competitive society and capitalism. An executive in a large, international company expresses the shift in value:

> One feature [of the Conservative Party] that strikes me very much—they are against the sort of British puritanism in that they recognize—as the Labour party doesn't—that if you want successful economic growth you must allow people to become millionaires. And thus you must allow rascals to become millionaires. You cannot close the loopholes and still retain the incentives. I feel this is a realistic view. [This means an acquisitive society?] It does. We've all become acquisitive. The only people who are not allowed to become acquisitive are the jolly rich.

> We are moving from an aristocratic society to a plutocratic society.

The Center group is more amorphous, but there are common threads in their self-characterizations. The word "radical," defined as seeking change, appears often. Doctrinaire ideology, whether conservative or socialist, is condemned. Humanitarian values and social reform are affirmed, but capitalism is accepted. In short, we see "liberalism," with all its ambiguities and tensions. In this sense, these are the most "American" of the Englishmen. We hear such phrases as "want more state action to increase equality of opportunity, income, wealth but fearful of encroachment on the individual"—"am a radical but accept capitalist society"—"not interested in ideology, just use state power to increase freedom and equality"—"like 'realists,' ideologies are useless, am a radical"—"don't believe in a 'New Jerusalem,' Labour is admirable but unrealistic to seek social equality, Tories are not good at righting specific wrongs"—"am a radical, meaning not necessarily bound by the past."

An executive with a large corporation is an active member of the Liberal Party. His entire world view seems to be shaped by a sympathy and empathy for the problems of others. He expressed a concern that society be based on human principles and mutual respect. His father was a chartered accountant in a provincial city, and, as a boy, he fully expected to step into the tight, comfortable professional world of his father and his associates. However, an Army experience, which is described below, opened up new possibilities to him, as he described it, and caused him to want to go to university, something he would not have done to be an accountant. He now sees his life as an executive in a nationally and internationally important firm as a much broader life than he would have otherwise lived. His choice of a business career and his "liberalism" are related. He wanted to get beyond his father's provincial, middle-class existence. He sees himself as more modern than that and therefore not a traditionalist. His experience in the Army, joined to what appears to be a generally sympathetic personality, makes him open to reform ideas. When asked why he was a member of the Liberal Party, he answered:

Basically because I don't believe in being doctrinaire. I believe you've got to have a strategy but I don't believe you should just work on an emotional framework and, come what may, tackle the problem. You've got to look at problems. You've got to have principles. But you shouldn't be too doctrinaire. This is where Liberals give people this sort of intellectual freedom.

Conservatism means a defender of the status quo, a traditionalist, for whom every change has got to be wrong. Socialism is the doctrine that the state knows best and that state control is the answer to all our problems with equality being the watchword. Liberalism is a feeling that change must and should occur and that the individual freedoms should be fought for, but not at the expense of society as a whole. I would link liberalism and radicalism very closely together.

Although I had a "public school" education—I was in the services two years before university—I didn't get a commission. This had an impact on me. I saw people without opportunities which I had doing better than I had done. This was one of the most fundamental things that happened to me. This brought me up with a jolt and made me start thinking freshly for the first time.

We can make some general statements about these ideologies:

(1) There are three distinct traditions, emphasizing respectively: equality, hierarchy, and opportunity.

(2) Each of these traditions also affirms "community"—i.e., a balance of individual claims within a unified society. But the emphasis is moving away from community and toward individuality, whether it be conservative economic individualism, liberal concern about breaking barriers to opportunity, or socialist turning away from collectivism.

(3) One could interpret these changes as a "convergence" of ideology on a consensus about liberal capitalism, but a more likely trend is an adaptation of old ideologies to new meanings and purposes. The Tory tradition is shedding some of its hierarchic and mystical features in a secular age, but certain principles seem likely to survive: skill at governing, hierarchy in the form of meritocracy. Radicals are seeking a new qualitative creed beyond the old quantitative socialism. They seek a new humanism beyond the acquisitive society. Liberals affirm parts of each of the other traditions, seeking both individuality and community.

(4) There is a congruence of themes in the expression of desired changes in English society and culture and in the changing themes of political ideology. Modernization as an idea cuts across their general ideas about England and informs each of the political traditions. There is emphasis upon loosening old structures and generating new sources of individuality and vitality into social life. The three different versions of the England to be, while shaped by different ideological histories, also share the common Benthamite spirit of the day.

## THE ROOTS OF BELIEF

A profession is a way of life and may therefore engender important values in those who practice it. People with different values might seek different professions as a means of acting on those values. Table 2 suggests

TABLE 2
### PROFESSION AND IDEOLOGY

|                | Left | Center | Right |
|----------------|------|--------|-------|
| Social science | 8    | 5      | 1     |
| Planner        | 3    | 6      | 1     |
| Lawyer         | 5    | 4      | 2     |
| Manager        | 2    | 4      | 5     |

a positive relationship between profession and general ideological predisposition, though not an ironclad link.

Social scientists and planners are conspicuous on the Left and managers, and to a lesser degree lawyers, are conspicuous on the Right. Managers are rare on the Left, and social scientists and planners are rare on the Right. All professions are liberally represented in the Center.

We can suggest plausible hypotheses to explain the rough relationship of ideology and profession. Planners and social scientists, who are also academics, are not directly rooted in a business civilization but, in fact, hold norms that often run counter to the dominant mores of that civilization. They seek service, not profit, and yet often feel materially cheated by the dominant ethos. They may also feel powerless in contrast to "establishments." They may very well have chosen their professions because of such values, which have then been reinforced. Businessmen, on the other hand, identify with the dominant values of liberal, capitalist society: productivity, affluence, material progress, competition. They are not particularly conservative in traditional ways and are, in fact, progressives and modernizers in their own lights. Careers in management are also likely to attract the kinds of people who love aggressiveness, competition, and the drive for material success. Lawyers, being more professionally independent than the others, can also be more ideologically independent because they can choose a way to practice law that will be congruent with their basic values.

However, such hypotheses about occupational choice and values do not explain those in the ideological center. Nor do they explain those in an ideological position which is the reverse of the majority of that of their professional counterparts. However, most of these positions on the ideological spectrum can be explained if we look at individual life histories. The role of professional choice as a consequence of prior values then falls into perspective along with the other formative influences in the development of an ideology. But occupation is primarily a dependent factor in that it either reflects prior values or the implicit ideological bias of a profession is nullified or offset by other factors (Parkin, 1968).

Ideology, as defined here, is part of the development of personality and serves important cognitive and moral purposes for individuals. Man is an inquiring, morally striving, and purposeful being.

One acquires an ideology in the process of developing stable world views in early life and young adulthood and adheres to it, but modifies that ideology over time. It becomes functional because it makes the world meaningful and gives purposes to social life. We try to construct how the ideologies of individuals developed out of their personal histories and how these beliefs are congruent with their present social roles. An ideology thus becomes a rich individual mosaic which is distorted if placed on scales and continua and given weights and numbers.

In the course of the interview, the subjects were asked to describe their social backgrounds, education, occupations, and the political loyalties and belief of their parents. They were asked to think about what effect such an early environment, including the kind of community and atmosphere in which they were raised, might have had on their own beliefs. There was discussion of their educational experience and their thoughts about it as a formative influence, including postgraduate education and travel abroad. And they were asked about their reasons for occupational choice. The interview thus elicited a picture of the ideological development of each subject. We have compared all these case histories in terms of assessments of the relative importance of the following six factors on the development of their mature world views:

(1) parents' politics
(2) parents' class status
(3) ethnic and religious identity
(4) educational experience
(5) young adult experience—e.g., working or studying abroad
(6) the effect of occupational milieu upon values

Common background experiences emerge which seem to have led to common ways of looking at the world. Those within each ideological group have been put into types suggesting that each ideological camp is a mixture of many intellectual, social, and moral strands within the society.

## THE ENGLISH LEFT

The first group on the Left is composed of four lawyers and one political scientist. All are Jews, who have a strong sense of marginality in English society and yet feel a deep stake in the tolerance of England.

A barrister illustrates processes present in the others. His father is a doctor who was a Communist fellow traveler in the 1930s and is now a Conservative. He is very conscious of his marginality in England as a Jew and links such an awareness to his radicalism: "One of the main reasons I'm a socialist is that I'm a passionate anti-conservative. I have such contempt for the conservative tradition; it comes from being in an outgroup."

He attended a public school and Cambridge, and then studied at an

American law school and worked in the civil rights movement in the American South when it was at the height of its idealism in the early 1960s. These two American experiences showed him what a lawyer could do for creative social change in a society, something that his English legal education had not suggested. He is one of the founders of the small English civil rights movement and is active as both lawyer and lobbyist in this regard.

All of this group attribute their radicalism to a sense of "marginality." However, the majority did not have radical parents. But three lawyers had American experiences which seem to have increased their sense of marginality and objectivity about English society, but also their awareness of things that needed to be and could be done in England, particularly drawing from innovative examples in American law.

The second type are heirs of the nonconformist conscience and its commitment to reform. Two are Welsh and one is English and from a Quaker background. One is a lawyer and the others an economist and a political scientist.

The Welsh lawyer describes his family as long adherents of Welsh liberalism and tells how he feels a bit foreign living and working in England. He has transferred his loyalty to the Labour Party and adds, "it is really anti-conservatism; that is the best way to explain party loyalty."

He has been active in race relations work with some of the lawyers in the first group.

The economist originally went to Africa as a pacifist to avoid military service and got interested in problems of economic development, which took him to graduate school in America. He sees both his pacifism and his radicalism as rooted in the nonconformist tradition of his family and adds, "I think I react more strongly against violent inequalities rather than for more equalities."

The third group comes from working-class socialist family backgrounds. Both are planners.

The first planner's father was a miner and semi-skilled worker who was strongly socialist, as was his mother. His parents "were very libertarian in their treatment of us; I was never beaten."

He then adds that he is an atheist because he is a libertarian. "You don't have a God but make your own morality. If children were freed from religions, we'd get a lot more liberal thinking."

He communicates strong resentments about social class in England, especially the public schools, and he himself attended a redbrick university. His work as a planner is in trying to restore economic and social vitality to working-class villages, especially mining towns.

The fourth cluster is from middle-class socialist family backgrounds. They are an economist and a planner.

The economist is the child of a nationally prominent family whose members have served in Labour governments. The planner's father was a scientist and businessman who is a socialist, and his grandfather was a Methodist lay-preacher "and a socialist fifty years ago, when it meant something."

The final group of six on the Left, two political scientists, two economists, and two managers, are all from comfortable middle-class backgrounds. The social scientists seem to be of the Left because of the kinds of problems that concern them in their professions. The two managers saw themselves as "radical" modernizers with a concern for both economic development and social equality.

## THE ENGLISH RIGHT

The first type consisted of six persons from middle-class backgrounds whose parents had conservative values and who have absorbed a certain amount of traditionalism of an "old Tory" variety, but who, because of strong personal ambition to succeed in careers of business, law, and politics, have emphasized achievement and competitive values for themselves and in their general world view.

A few examples will illustrate.

A manager with a large industrial corporation grew up in a small village in Surrey, where his family had lived for hundreds of years. His parents are strongly Conservative, and his father, a plumber, is president of the local British Legion. He attended the local grammar school and Cambridge on a scholarship. Trained as a scientist, he worked in the government scientific civil service for a time and found it to be a hopeless, do-nothing bureaucracy. Industry, with its stress on results, pleases him much more. There is nothing of the old Tory about him in the sense of aristocratic paternalism and noblesse oblige. Rather, he is a combination of working-class and middle-class achievement conservative in his ideas.

A much more traditional figure is the son of a family who have been brewers in the south of England for two hundred years. As he said, "We are country gentry and therefore Tories." Educated at public school and Oxford, he entered his father's business in the city but was at the time a temporary civil servant. Although he is committed to "modernization," his traditionalism comes through:

I remember reading in the paper that a cotton textile management was complaining that it was impossible to get the local workers to work five shifts to keep the new machines working twenty-four hours a day, seven days a week, throughout the year. To which my instinctive reaction was . . . why the hell should people get up in the middle of the night to work the textile machines if they didn't want to? . . . Either we persuade our workers in the North to work five shifts a week . . . or we lose out internationally, and our standard of living goes down, and so forth. It's really a choice facing us, to which I'm slightly skeptical. I think it's a very sad and serious thing. And a very sad commentary on modern life. Poor Lancastrians have to work in the small hours of the morning if the Japanese do it, not because they want to. . . . I think there is a danger in worshipping production and subordinating literally everything to increasing and accelerating the rate of growth in national products. I think this can be overdone, and I think there are signs of this being overdone in the states. I think Galbraith certainly had a point there.

One sees the tension between ascription and achievement in the following:

I am rather conscious of my background and in a way I wish I'd been born in the suburbs, a much more anonymous situation than in fact I am. . . . My family has lived in this house for two hundred years. We are—well, not the squires actually—but we have a large farm and we are at the squire end of the typically old English village community. There is no doubt this has made an enormous difference to me in a way to set me apart from the more active middle class. And, in a way, I rather regret it. I feel if one had been born in the suburbs and lived in the suburbs, one would have had much wider range of choices, friends, and interest, and so forth. Nevertheless, such is the quality of life I've been brought up with that it's not everybody who can live on a farm as I have done, in lovely country. . . . There again, I'm torn between the two.

The second type of conservative seems to have been primarily influenced by adult experience and occupation to be conservative, although solid middle-class background is present in each case. They are a planner, a barrister, and an economist.

The planner's father was a businessman, though without strong political views. A graduate of a redbrick university, this planner has a very strong "achievement" orientation and feels that socialism has gone overboard on social welfare, and that the Tories are more capable "modernizers." His strongest commitment in planning is to the increase of technical proficiency throughout the profession, but this does not distinguish him from left-wing planners.

The lawyer is a Jew who attended school and university with one of the lawyer-radicals and had a comparable experience with an American law school. However, out of this background, he has become a Conservative

Parliamentary candidate. His values are those of a Center-Right liberal, perhaps, but there was no mention of consciousness of marginality nor of resentment against an establishment. He is seeking to join it as a modernizer.

The economist is from a lower-middle-class background but has become identified with a prominent Tory politician and at the time was working for the party central office. His values are those of the modernizing conservative.

### THE ENGLISH CENTER

Those in the Center fall into two groups—the cross-pressured and the liberals. The former have predispositions from both Left and Right in their backgrounds and have developed strategies of compromise. The latter seem influenced by a clear background tradition.

The phenomenon of cross-pressure is nicely illustrated in a manager in an international oil firm who is of working-class background. His mother left school at age twelve to work in a factory. His father has been a porter, van driver, and clerk who has never earned more than twelve pounds a week and will always live in public housing. He wanted to be a carpenter but could never afford to wait out the apprenticeship time:

> He feels he has little to show for his life except his children. This is one reason why I am so concerned with human resources being used. His have not been.

This has led to many views:

> I'm very critical of things like the public schools, of the inbred status and self-preserving policies of certain status bodies like the city livery companies, the law, Eton, All Souls College, Oxford, the club land of Pall Mall.

He himself served as an army officer, where he says that he acquired considerable social polish, attended Oxford and then "went into oil." His dominant concern is the importance of creating a modern society and economy:

> A lot of people's energies are devoted to preserving these sorts of distinctions between people where they could be employed in being a bit more useful or productive generally. . . . What really gets my goat is the sort of middle- to upper-middle-class attitude whereby the trade unions are not even a necessary evil, where events in

Rhodesia are regarded as scuttling the British cousins there—all this nonsense—the coffee party, bridge party, gin drinking, stockbroker approach. I know these are clichés, but they are very strong, self-perpetuating societies which are buttressed by public school education, by the closed societies of the golf clubs. I find them terribly enervating.

For reasons like these, he does not line up with the Conservative Party, the higher civil service, or any "establishments." He supports the Labour Party, a force for "modernization" of the society, in education, science, technology, and much else.

Other stories are not dissimilar: the son of a miner who attended Cambridge; the son of reactionary Tory parents of high status who first learned about social equality at the Harvard Business School and has become a fanatic modernizer; the son of a newspaper reporter who attended a public school and feels torn between the radicalism of his father's views and his own personal conservatism acquired in part at school; a conservative businessman who supports the Labour Party because he sees it as the best vehicle for modernization.

In the second group, all the factors are working in the same direction, toward a moderate, reforming liberalism: the planner who comes from a nationally prominent family of academics who have held high office in first Liberal and then Labour governments, but the essential outlook of which is that of a slightly paternalistic and very earnest reformism; a social scientist from a working-class family whose "socialism" is strictly the desire to have "more jam" for everyone, with little thought of utopia and contempt for socialist intellectuals; a social scientist from a Liberal, pacifist, nonconformist background and American graduate education, who is interested in improving British economics; a social scientist from a Liberal, Quaker family, a lawyer from one of the oldest and most prominent Liberal families; a barrister whose parents are doctors and who sees himself as a "radical" in his willingness to question tradition; and finally a lawyer whose father was a schoolmaster, who attended public school and Oxford on scholarship, who is a "very modern meritocrat" in his ideas.

## POLITICAL SUBCULTURES

There are no striking differences in social backgrounds among Left, Right, and Center. As Table 3 shows, the great majority are from middle-class families and attended either Oxford or Cambridge. About half of each group attended public schools. The totals vary because of uneven responses.

**TABLE 3**
**SOCIAL BACKGROUND**

|  | Left | Right | Center |
|---|---|---|---|
| **Parents' Class** | | | |
| Working | 2 | 1 | 4 |
| Middle | 14 | 7 | 15 |
| **Education** | | | |
| Public school | 6 | 6 | 9 |
| Grammar | 8 | 3 | 10 |
| Oxford or Cambridge | 13 | 7 | 9 |
| Redbrick | 2 | 1 | 4 |
| University of London | 1 | – | 3 |
| No university | – | 1 | – |
| **Religion** | | | |
| Protestant | 11 | 6 | 19 |
| Jew | 5 | 1 | – |
| Catholic | – | 1 | – |

We are thus looking at three very diffuse political subcultures within the English middle classes, which are carried by families and which coexist within the same educational and professional institutions. These subcultures are most clear with those of the Left and Right, ranging from "marginal men" to country gentry or nonconforming reformer to the Tory meritocrat. We are given a picture of great richness and variety in middle-class society.

## GOVERNMENT

A number of academicians, political reformers, and politicians have begun to see virtues in the American system of government which might be transplanted to England. British government is seen by its critics as too hierarchical and secretive. The Cabinet makes decisions in secret, without the benefit of sufficiently wide discussion in Parliament and the nation. The House of Commons then debates such decisions in mock partisan fashion, contributing little to the quality of the final policy. The virtue of party government and party discipline, so long admired abroad, is thus seen as a defect because it does not encourage sufficient real debate about policy. The parties play political games in the House of Commons, but Parliament makes little real contribution to policy-making (Crick, 1965).

English reformers have thus come to envy the greater openness and fragmentation of American government and have suggested that the powers of Parliament and of M.P.s vis-à-vis the government should be enhanced. Experiments in this direction have been conducted (Mackintosh, 1971). In fact, reform of Parliament has been for some time the conventional wisdom among innovators in Britain. The leading idea is that the governmental policy-making process needs to be more open, less secretive, and more fluid. Government is thought to have made a number of decisions of poor quality in recent years because Cabinet Ministers and high civil servants have not been required to justify their policies before decisions were made. The themes of secrecy and amateurism are often linked—i.e., British policy makers, especially civil servants, are often "amateurs," and therefore they are secretive. It follows that one way to make them more expert is to open their work up to Parliamentary scrutiny.

The most frequently suggested reform is the specialized Parliamentary committee which would scrutinize the preparation of legislation and the implementation of laws. Such committees, served by expert staffs, would extract the necessary public discussion of policy options from ministers and civil servants before decisions are made and brought to Parliament as legislation. It is suggested that specialist committees, working in an atmosphere of publicity, could give the public a sense that Parliament mattered in the policy-making process and therefore strengthen a popular allegiance to representative government.

Resistance to such reforms of the House is strong among those who interpret the role of Parliament to be primarily that of a partisan debating chamber which exists to continue the electoral battle between elections and therefore requires no real policy-making functions. Parliamentary reform is likely to be most popular with the kinds of people interviewed in this study: politically minded experts who are not themselves in Parliament.

The subjects were asked if they were generally satisfied with the way Parliamentary institutions were functioning. Thirty-four said no. Seven said yes. Three had no clear opinion, and two were not asked.

Twenty-three of those who were critical favored the expansion of the specialized committees to provide for more openness between government and Parliament in policy discussion. Twenty-one of these made the general argument that the role of Parliament vis-à-vis the government needed to be enhanced to ensure a greater quality of policy discussion.

A number of those advocating reform based their views on personal experience with the House of Commons. A manager working temporarily for a government department which was then in the midst of a public controversy said that he favored a more open committee system because, "I would like to be able to defend———practices more openly." A lawyer and Labour candidate for Parliament who is active as a lobbyist in race relations commented:

> As a lobbyist I discovered that M.P.s are grateful to whoever can give them information. That's how we got the race relations law. The absence of some kind of committee system is bad. They don't develop expertise. There is no sustained public scrutiny of policy. It comes only after the decisions are taken. It should come before.

A barrister and former Conservative backbencher who has since returned to the House, spoke of his experiences:

> It was an enormously time-consuming, time-wasting, frustrating place in which to work in opposition. No doubt as a forum in which to achieve ministerial office, if you get there reasonably quickly, it's a satisfying sort of limbo. But as an institution to do whatever it's meant to achieve, it's plainly not satisfactory, But, it's far less easy to see what is to be done about it. At question time, for example—since you can never ask a second question on the same topic—you can ask a minister whether he would now be kind enough to answer the question you first put to him. It's a great charade for the most part.

> I'd agree with that [specialized committees] as being probably worthwhile. But I'm more concerned about the fundamentals of the structure. Query—whether the Prime Minister's power of dissolution and irregular elections and the fact that all votes are votes of confidence are not the most disabling things. The complete fusion of the executive and the legislature, which is avoided in the American system—I know the Americans will readily identify deficiencies in this. . . . If in fact the executive proposes but the legislature in fact decided in the chaotic way the Congress reviews the President's proposals . . . there is a genuine conflict. Merely to have chaps sitting on committees quizzing top civil servants is to increase the focus of criticism to some extent, to introduce a bit more light into it. But it doesn't necessarily introduce the element of conflict and persuasion which is introduced if the government can't be certain of their Parliamentary majority. On the other hand, to work the right trick to change that so as not [to] frustrate the whole thing altogether is exceedingly difficult.

> I think the role of the individual politician is very narrow and frustrating in this country compared to the extent to which it seems—on the grass is greener theory—that the individual congressman and senator can establish an individual position and contribute and be respected for doing that.

He admires the American model, but pulls back from copying. However, he goes farther than anyone else in challenging the authority of the government to get its own way with legislation. The more common view is that expressed by a planner, that greater expertise and scrutiny of government by members of Parliament would give informal influence to parliamentarians:

> I think the number of M.P.s, the division of powers between Parliament and the executive is reasonable. . . . On the other hand, I really do think that—and all the financial scandals from years ago over defense and other expenditures—I think it goes to reinforce the view that we have got to make our legislators and controllers better equipped and thereby more professional. . . . I don't think about more power or enough power [for Parliament] . . . you should see the Civil Service hop when a Parliamentary question gets asked. I'm on an advisory council to the government, and I know how these things make them hop . . . and the few select committees we have got are pretty powerful. . . . Oh no, they have got enough powers, but simply haven't got the resources to use those powers.

A concern that the peculiar virtues of Parliament as a general debating forum be retained also runs through the comments. One economist, a former civil servant, expressed his admiration of American "professionalism" compared to British "amateurism," and then added:

> It is one of the most fascinating problems in social engineering precisely how you reconcile, especially in this increasingly technological world, the need for the professional scientific approach with giving priority ultimately to human values.

When asked for an illustration, he replied:

> Reforming Parliament is one obvious case. On the one hand, there's a strong desire to modernize and reform Parliament, have select committees with a staff, more research associates, etc. . . . like Senate committees perhaps. . . . On the other hand, there is the fear that perhaps some traditional M.P.s express, but I think has something in it, that if you go too far and give exclusive priority to this, you are in danger of losing the all-round virtue of Parliament in its sessions of the whole House, question time, and so on, in defending the liberties of the individual and upholding some sort of basic traditions and principles of British life. Logically, there is no contradiction between these two, and people might argue that this can only be done, liberties protected, by basic reform . . . but it's a point to keep one's eye on in that there is a risk that everyone becomes so occupied with their specialist committees and their research and so on that some basic rights are forgotten—e.g., there is no committee on fundamental rights, and we don't have a Supreme Court. In a highly professional environment in which you can't do or say

anything without the weight of evidence or authority behind you, it is more difficult to talk off the top of one's head about basic liberties.

So while in favor of reform for more expertise, he seeks a balance with an older tradition of general discussion peculiar to the practices of an organic institution which is not fragmented into specialist bodies.

Six of those who were dissatisfied called for mild procedural reforms like loosening of party discipline. The tone was that of criticism of the subservience of M.P.s to the government. Four called for "better people" in Parliament—for example, businessmen wishing for more businessmen in politics. One called for an even stronger executive.

Seven answered that they were satisfied. A political scientist spoke for their traditional view:

> It all depends what you think the proper function of Parliament should be. To me, the function of Parliament is to provide opportunities for debate and talk, opportunities for the government to explain its position, for the opposition to force the government out into the open and explain their position—informing the electorate so that when the election comes they can judge. . . . I see Parliament as a speaking chamber. I don't want it to have any more than that because, with my knowledge of British government, I see the center of British government as administration, as the executive, consisting of ministers and civil servants. . . . I don't want limits put on administrative and executive action. A lot of the reforms—e.g., select committees—are devised to check the administration, to hinder administrative decisions and political decisions, generally reinforcing conservatism, giving more and more opportunities to professional and vested interests to clog and delay.

He is not so much in disagreement with the reformers as he thinks, because they are not really interested in challenging the authority of the executive. Rather, the common argument is that more open discussion of government policy options by Parliamentary committees during the policy-making stage would improve the quality of that policy. Whether such a model of reform is compatible with the system of partisan government with strong lines of discipline is an open question. However, as we saw, even this pattern is suspect. These professional experts seem to think of policy resolution in more ad hoc terms.

## POWER OF CENTRAL GOVERNMENT

The same pattern of search for new balances also appears with regard to the power of central government and restraining institutions. The question was: "Would you say a few things about the power of central government in Britain, whether it is too strong or too weak, too centralized or not centralized enough?" One was not asked. Eight thought the situation was fine as it was, by which they meant strong centralized government. One thought central government was too weak. Thirteen thought strong central government was all right, but favored a variety of different kinds of restraints on its powers—e.g., greater effort to take account of public opinion through surveys, a written bill of rights, Parliamentary committees. These people did not raise the issue of local government. The 23 who did raise the issue of local government repeated a common theme that central government has become unwieldy, has in many ways lost touch with people at the grass roots, that communication links are not good, that there is more information at the center than can be usefully used. The general formula proposed for solution of these problems was a greater devolution of the administration of central government, but without destroying the overall coherence, power, and authority of that central government. The theme was much like that with regard to Parliamentary committees—i.e., that there was need for more public discussion of issues between government and the restraining bodies but that the authority of the center should not be impaired. Again, there was an assumption of the reasonableness of authority, that once issues could be ventilated and objections and initiatives raised at a lower level, those in central authority would listen and be responsive.

As might be expected, the planners were the most keen on devolution of the authority of central government because it directly affected their work, but they also felt that comprehensive national planning was vital, so a balance of some kind was needed. Here is one planner who reflects not only the attitude of the planners but of those who felt that central government had, in the past, been too restrictive and paternalistic:

There's a terrible paternalism—"yes, we'll let you decide so far, but really in the end we—the central government machine—really ought to look after you in your own interests, old chap." This is a paternalism which was less appropriate in a less educated and less sophisticated society one hundred years ago. [Does this attitude and the acceptance of it give British government greater authority?] I think it does. If you've got a very highly educated elite mandarin class in government, which you undoubtedly have, their continuance is fostered by a feeling that paternalism is O.K. I think this is on the wane, but the time in which I grew up was one in which paternalism was still very strong, and people acquiesced to it—said those chaps who had been to public school and good universities really know what's good for us—it's the old tradition of touching your forelock to the leader in the community. We are becoming—not because we are copying North America, but because of similar trends in education in a society as well as political history—we are becoming more pluralist in our attitude ... there's going to be a very much more powerful devolution to people who are now very, very much better educated. They are consumers of public services more than they ever were before. And they won't tolerate this.

However, it was clear from discussion that he wanted the continuance of strong central government. His goal was greater authority to local governments in strictly local matters, and greater responsiveness and communication by central government with all groups affected by it.

A political scientist gives the dominant view:

I do have a strong feeling that people ought to have a real say in certain kinds of issues. I'm a supporter of some kind of elected regional authority, for example ... but I don't on the other hand want that kind of decentralization to make it impossible to take the very tough central decisions on planning and so on. ... I don't think it is impossible to combine some very genuine liberties with a tough exercise of authority. Partly, that is a question of your style of exercising authority ... if you prepare the ground sufficiently, if you are open to criticism, if you don't seem dishonest about it, then I think, certainly in this country, you can get away with taking tough decisions.

So while the planner rejects rule by "mandarins," both he and the political scientist suggest that a strong central responsive authority must prevail. This is an old principle in a new formulation.

The theme of need for increased "openness" is dominant. But this openness is to exist within a framework of authority and capacity for action by government. Openness is seen as an instrumental value which will actually enhance governmental authority. It was put best by a political scientist who has written and thought much on the subject:

There might be some grounds for thinking that an increased openness of government might lead to superior results. I mean results built on the sense of being able to ascertain more clearly what it is people want and need, and also to ascertain more clearly whether people's behavior can be influenced in directions that governments and the rest think are desirable. ... It seems to have been rather lost sight of by governments who seem on the whole anxious to have something that they may call authority that enables them to be able to do things without having to explain why they do a thing.

The point is simply that "openness" will make British government more, not less, effective. There is perception of a functional imperative. But that imperative must be met within the broad framework of the traditional authority of government to act.

Harry Eckstein (1962) suggests that, historically, there has been a tension and collaboration between the energizing, centralizing, initiating forces in British government and the passive, checking, consenting forces. This style of authority has been seen in the various relations of King and Parliament, Cabinet and Parliament, and government and nation over many centuries. Whenever the balance has seemed in danger of being upset, in either direction, gradual institutional change develops to set it right according to the original implicit formula. Thus, the Cabinet replaced the King as the effective executive, and Parliament remained a consenting body. The development of mass parties forged links between government and nation in terms of the original formula. The perceived imbalance in Britain today is a concern that central government and the executive may have become top-heavy, cut off from adequate communication with potential critics and with those affected by policies. Elite secrecy has ceased to be functional. Decisions need greater legitimizing.

The search for a balance between tradition and change in the character of the society was one of the clearest themes expressed by the English in their discussions of national values. The baby was not to be thrown out with the bath. The "nice" qualities of Britain were not to be sacrificed. We see an institutional counterpart to this cultural theme in the ideas about government. Parliament is to be reformed, central government made more responsive, and the executive more open, but in terms of an implicit normative model of balance between authority and restraint. There seems to be an implicit search for a new formula which will reaffirm the old balances. It is a demand for coherence and containment. It is assumed that national institutions are to bring authority, unity, and accomplishment to the society. These institutions must be open to currents from the community, but they give the society its coherence. This is not a model of checks and balances in dynamic equilibrium. Rather, balance is seen as a complementary fusion of opposites. The formula of change is feeling one's way to new balances in old institutions.

## SUMMING UP

We have found a congruence of themes about the desired directions of change with regard to society and culture, political ideology and governmental institutions. The society needs to become less tradition-bound and dynamic. Ideologies need to combine old values with the goal of a more dynamic, modernizing society. Institutions need to be more open, more decentralized, more responsive to publics, and more capable of policy innovation. In short, we find a common Benthamite ideology about desired social change in Britain which cuts across ideological, social, and occupational differences. There is a commitment to modernization.

The social background factors which help explain specific political ideology in these individuals may also contribute to their general Benthamite radicalism. Their social backgrounds may have caused them to feel certain tensions with the dominant ethos of elite culture in England and to have therefore embraced the Benthamite counter-currents. Those on the Left who feel themselves to be marginal men do reject establishment values in part, in favor of radical ideas. The heirs to the nonconformist conscience find the new puritanism of modernization congenial. Those on the Center who feel "cross-pressured" between humble backgrounds and occupational success in modern sectors have little use for ascriptive elites and values. The strong liberal reformers of the Center come from families and backgrounds which have been carriers of Benthamite values of different hues over time and are therefore much at home in reform ideas. More difficult to explain in terms of social background are those of working-class socialist families or middle-class conservative families who have turned away from traditional versions of those faiths and espouse different versions of the gospel of modernization. They are expressing the dominant ideas in their traditions at the current time.

However, social background might provide only predispositions toward Benthamite radicalism. Perhaps other factors are necessary to stimulate this bent, such as age, social position, and profession. We will consider a wider range of hypotheses after we have looked at their professional lives.

## CHAPTER III
## PROFESSIONALS, SOCIETY, AND GOVERNMENT

We will find a congruence of themes about reform of the professions and development of new professional roles with the reform themes expressed in Chapter II:

(1) insistence upon the development and application of new and better techniques of knowledge and problem-solving to professional skills;

(2) stress on the need to develop new social roles for the several professions; this is one expression of a larger commitment to a greater structural differentiation of elite roles in institutions and a greater horizontal mobility of elites across institutional boundaries;

(3) adherence to American professional models as sources of innovative ideas.

We can develop a model of the role of the innovative professional acting in a time of rapid, but orderly social and institutional change in a society. The model posits a close link between general currents of social change and changing professional norms with each influencing the other:

(1) general dissatisfaction in innovative segments of the society with aspects of the traditional culture and institutions;

(2) professionals in those segments perceive a conflict between traditional professional norms and goals and new tasks and knowledge;

(3) a congruence of directions of general institutional and cultural reform and directions of professional role change with each stimulating the other;

(4) use of professional roles as vehicles for innovation in six ways:
  (a) cross-cultural borrowing with regard to professional knowledge or roles
  (b) introducing new knowledge into the profession
  (c) redefining the social roles of the profession
  (d) developing new roles for the profession within institutions which are also undergoing innovation
  (e) change in the general relationships of professional and other elite roles in institutions
  (f) change in the character of the culture as the professions introduce new knowledge and values;

(5) new patterns of authority develop as a result of new elite role patterns and new uses and disseminations of knowledge.

## PLANNERS[1]

British government and society have been very supportive of comprehensive planning since World War II and this practice has its roots in a number of social facts (Altshuler, 1965):

(1) There is an acute sense of land shortage on a tiny, heavily urbanized island.

(2) Capitalist ideas about unrestricted free market forces as the chief factor in the development of the urban environment have not been strong in England. Both aristocratic Tory notions of preserving the

countryside and creating elegant cities and socialist ideas about decent communities have constricted the operation of the market.

(3) The unitary character of British government has permitted national government to set land use policies to which local governments have had to adhere.

(4) Political elites of all ideologies and parties have believed in comprehensive planning. As a result, planners have had considerable support from their political "masters."

(5) Ministers and civil servants exercise great discretionary power, and publics have been trusting because such powers are not abused. This has permitted governments to put strong constraints on land use.

(6) World War II, with its great destruction, was a watershed in the national determination to rebuild the urban environment.

Postwar British governments have built a larger number of "New Towns," attempted to integrate economic development and physical planning, and have followed general policies of opposition to uncontrolled urban sprawl. Planners have had strong levers of control over land use in law and administrative practice.

However, British planning practice has been criticized for being too elitist. Minister, civil servants, and planners have decided how people should live. There has also been concern that physical planning has been overemphasized at the expense of economic and social plans. Architects have perhaps had too much say to the exclusion of social science. And planning as a process is said to have been so authoritative that it has been difficult for government to make adjustments in plans to new social trends (Foley, 1963).

The ten English planners interviewed were receptive to such criticisms and were trying to find ways to modify their received tradition of comprehensive planning in order to make it more effective. The chief intellectual influence was American planning literature, written primarily by academics, about the need to bring cybernetic and systems approaches into planning. This is accompanied as well by a greatly increased emphasis in American planning upon social as well as physical plans. The planner in a Model Cities project, for example, is seen as a social change agent. These ideas appeal to English planners because they offer ways to criticize traditional British planning and yet revitalize it.

The ten planners worked in a variety of settings: two for the London County Council, three directing subregional plans, one as a county planning officer, one for a metropolitan area, one in the ministry of Housing and Local Government, one in rural regional planning, and one with a varied career as a practitioner who had recently become an academic.

They were asked two questions which led to lengthy discussions: first, what changes they saw in the planning profession in England and what they thought about them; second, whether they had a goal of an "ideal city" and whether it was a good thing for a planner to have.

The themes that were mentioned in answer to the first question in order of frequency were:

(1) move from emphasis on physical design and land use toward greater attention to the city as a framework of open-ended systems, social, economic, physical, and so on—6

(2) development of better planning technique—3

(3) decline of elitism—1

Here is a planner for the London County Council:

British planning was internationally famous for its civic design type planning—e.g., the New Towns. I'm not so sure that this adds up to all that much. For example, we have built a ring of New Towns around London at a cost of x million pounds. Supposing that money was spent in London itself. What alternative ways were there of dealing with these situations which weren't even thought about? We were stuck with the civic design thing, the Garden City thing.

I favor a systems view of planning, the idea of a city as a system rather than as an architectural artifact.

The general impression around is that the Americans understand how it works much better than we do but are incapable of doing anything about it. We can do something about it but don't understand how it works.

The director of a subregional planning study is widely regarded as the most innovative young planner. After he had mentioned the revolt against the design tradition, I asked him what had caused the change, in his view:

The rockbottom cause is better young people coming into the profession, in two ways . . . the "pure" planning courses have been pushing more and more people like myself into the profession. A far better education than a lot of the old guard had. Two, people from other original skills like economics and the other social sciences have come in. They have put their nasty little L.S.E. minds onto this problem and said: "What the hell are you chaps trying to do anyway?" and forced the old guard to ask this. . . . Not to be ignored is the influence of what has been happening in North America, from the earliest transportation plans, an impressive array of new thinking and practice, at first seemingly wholly irrelevant to British conditions and problems. I've played a little part in trying to convince people that they were by no means irrelevant but were very highly relevant. They were universal—deal with the nature of human settlement systems.

And then, in an indictment of older traditions of planning:

Both he [older style of planner] and the politicians were part of a much smaller elite minority who were working the act together. It was a double act. Sir Patrick Abercrombie and the old London County Council . . . people from the same social background who thought, "Yes, what these workers want is lovely new towns, set beyond the greenbelt. What they want is nice groups of flats in the middle of London and a jolly good transport system." Well, maybe they did, but no one ever took serious trouble to find out, neither the politician nor the planner, or to test serious options. They were effective because they were working a very good double act.

It's paternalistic to a very high degree . . . the goals which are implicit in this thing are physical-form goals. As Mel Webber [innovative American planner, a personal acquaintance] and others point out, people are happy for thousands of different reasons. Why should we be so arrogant? It is the architectural background of the British planning profession which is that much different from the American planning profession for that reason. The idea is that you make people happy through giving them physical forms to live in. . . . You tend to overlook all the other aspects of the urban system which really do make people unhappy. Perhaps what they really want is more money or greater choice of work.

I asked him what his professional goals as a planner were, and he answered:

Far superior technique in the narrow sense. . . . Far greater responsiveness of these techniques in the service of objectives to be explored with the consumer. . . . Far higher levels of intellect among the professionals. . . . It's the diametrical opposite of woefully sloppy, nontechnique, nonunderstanding of a terribly paternalistic attitude, the absurd shibboleths largely developed inside the planning profession—e.g., that "Greenbelts are good for you."

In response to the second question about the value of a model of the "ideal city," all rejected it if it meant ideal in terms of physical form. The theme of the city as an open system or systems was again expressed. However, all pointed out that the planner still had an obligation to have personal values about what a city should be and that he should make efforts to get politicians and publics to consider the goals involved in planning.

They reported an increased awareness that the development of the city was shaped by processes such as the market, which the planner could not easily control, and the conclusion was drawn that planning itself must be open-ended and flexible. Yet, at the same time, there was a commitment to comprehensive planning. Here is a regional planner who is critical of the reliance of American planning upon the market to shape the central character of the city:

> The free society, the uncontrolled legislative framework there, in which you try to simulate what will happen rather than to guide it, is a quite different situation from ours. . . . The free market is a myth. It doesn't really work like that and let us not try to pretend that the best way of achieving satisfactory results is through the free market. We've got to find out what is happening in the mixed market, not the free market, and then we've got to guide it into the directions we think better. . . . We've got to know what's happening. We've got to monitor it all the time, and we've got to be guiding it in the direction you want to go.

A planner of high rank in the Ministry of Housing and Local Government put things into focus: "The ideal city is now conceived, not in physical terms, but as a city that works as a system."

The city was seen as an open-ended entity encompassing many social factors besides the physical. And the implicit normative goal was for balance between factors in the "system" and for securing agreement on what balances were to be sought. We see this in the planner earlier described as among the most "innovative" who was asked, as a spokesman for the systems approach what was added by it.

> You can plug into this intellectual framework the real tough tools of the trade like forecasting in a spatial sense—i.e., what settlement will occur if we do this or that? The mere fact that you say "if" brings into context the goals and objectives of society because when you say "if" you therefore beg the question to the political side of the operation—do you want to do that sort of thing? Do you want there to be no agricultural land here at all? Well, then—going through the systems framework into the hardware of spatial prediction, this is the sort of shape and size of city you would tend to get. This is the sort of public investment program you have to be prepared to mount.

> I think it's a tremendous advantage—it goes a long, long way towards the hardware side and also it brings within one context the social purposes which these things are supposed to serve. There has been a terrible, confused battle raging for years here and in North America too about what is a planner and when is he an economist or an

architect, etc.? Why people find it so difficult to communicate and decide what their roles are in planning is that they haven't had a common language. To see the city as a particular kind of system enables one guy to say, "Ah yes, I see now where I come in to clarify this particular kind of connection system, I'm a transport man" or "I am a housing economist, so I'm talking about one kind of component in the system." The aesthetic guy says "Oh yes, I can see I'm dealing with something which is more comprehensive with respect to the system, but it's only part of it. It's the qualitative dimension of the whole."

He then went on to say that the planner should have goals of his own for the city, but that his chief role was:

to aid in invention for the client group. He can point out to the client group what options are open to them which lie outside their everyday experience. He might be able to point out that they can have a transportation system which they had never conceived as possible. This is not quite the same thing as forcing his own values onto the client. It's enlarging their range of explorations. I was very impressed with Altshuler's point that the planner can enlarge the frame of reference.

Notice in his comments references to two American writers on planning, Melvin Webber and Alan Altshuler.

These planners have not so much turned their backs on traditional British planning styles as they are seeking to modernize those styles by grafting on new approaches and softening the emphasis upon physical design and paternalism. The older approaches are rejected; social science and systems analysis are added. The old commitment to comprehensive planning is retained. There is less certainty about the shape of the ideal city, but there is a strong belief that planning should be comprehensive in terms of people's values and goals. An ideal city that works as a system has replaced the ideal city of physical form. American planning methods appeal much more than American planning goals, but there is more awareness than in the past of the importance of spontaneous social and market processes, and this is very strong in American planning.

We can see their innovativeness at work in their practice. The two planners for the London County Council were working on a new long-range comprehensive plan for greater London and were particularly concerned that the plan express the social and economic "tradeoffs" between different land use patterns. The three subregional planners were trying to develop systems techniques in the plans for their areas, again so that alternative futures might be debated. The metropolitan and county planners were also applying new ideas of open-ended flexible plans. The planner in Whitehall was most concerned to get new planning ideas and techniques out to planners in the field. The academic planner was studying how people actually develop and revise planning goals over time. And the rural planner was working on new ways to revitalize villages and towns.

All were contributing to innovation in the degree to which they were using new "hardware" in planning and shrank back from the strong normative certainties of the previous generation of planners and posited a more open-ended search for goals. The full outline of new professional-institutional roles cannot be drawn without a much more detailed analysis of actual role behavior of these individuals. One would have to look at the reactions of politicians, other civil servants, publics. How do these other actors respond to planner styles that emphasize more sophisticated methodologies and theories and more flexible notions about goals than older planners? Must these other actors adjust their styles as well? Eight of these planners were involved in comprehensive planning of one kind or another, particularly new kinds of regional planning or comprehensive metropolitan planning. It would be interesting to ask how their role behavior differs from that of the planners who planned the New Towns and the expansion of greater London after the war. Scholars who have looked at these plans and planners in research done in the 1950s describe the planning as heavily architectural and physical in tone and as definitely elitist and in that sense congruent with the role definitions of politicians and civil servants (Rodwin, 1956). Perhaps the entire set of leadership roles in planning—politicians, civil servants, and planners—is shifting in new directions along the lines of the themes suggested here. An illustration of this comes from one planner working on a long-range plan:

the politicians here are just not used at all to planners knocking on their door and saying, "Look, I want a long talk with you guys about what sort of plan you are trying to get out of me." And they say, "But we're paying you to tell us." And, I say, "No, you're paying me to study physical form, the location of activities, and I'm asking you to what ends is this being done?"

It is the intention of these innovators that the new planning approaches strengthen the capabilities of planning and governmental authority by making plans more flexible and open to information as well as by adding new powers of technique. But these suggested new approaches to planning could also weaken the authoritative stance of professional planners and diminish the self-confidence of both planners and civil servants and political leaders about the rights and wrongs of urban development. If planners are less certain of either their knowledge or their values, they will surely communicate this to civil servants and politicians. Clear notions of the good city, surrounded by greenbelts and viewed as an architectural entity, will decline, but what will take their place? A systems cybernetic view of planning with open-ended, flexible plans may permit a great deal more politics and interest-group tugging and hauling than has been the case in the past era of comprehensive planning.

However, these trends in English planning are shared by planning in other modern nations, including the United States. Planners have come to realize that they lack perfect knowledge, normative certainty, and political authority to impose fixed, physical master plans on reality. Planning must become cybernetic in its open-endedness. The challenge is to somehow get beyond both the rigid masterplan and uncoordinated, ad hoc, fragmented incrementalism to new kinds of purposive, coordinated, and yet open and flexible planning. These English planners seem headed in this direction. For better or worse, they must forsake past planning styles and develop new ones.

## LAWYERS

The profession is divided into two branches, solicitors and barristers. The barristers are the acknowledged "elite" who do all the pleading in the higher courts, form the pool from which the judiciary come, and are better educated in terms of having university degrees. The majority of barristers in the country are in London, practicing in central courts, with chambers in the four Inns of Court. The solicitors are, for the most part, general practitioners who have historically been legal advisers to middle-class families.

Neither branch of the profession requires a university degree for admittance. There are no graduate law schools similar to those in America. A student may read law at a university, but this involves Roman law, jurisprudence, constitutional history, and basic common law subjects. Actual legal training comes by an apprenticeship system in lawyers' offices or chambers, supplemented by evening lectures at the Inns of Court of the Law Society (Solicitor's Guild), usually given by practitioners. There is no professional counterpart to the American legal academic who moves freely and with zest among university, private practice, and government.

Clients may approach only solicitors directly. If they need to go to court, their solicitor takes them to see a barrister, is present during all interviews, and is present in court. Both lawyers receive a fee.

Lawyers play a more limited number of social roles in England than in most modern industrial societies, and the law plays a less important role in social life than in most other nations. There are many reasons for this (Abel-Smith and Stevens, 1967):

(1) The constitution is unwritten and develops by convention rather than legal rules. Constitutional issues are therefore settled outside the courts as political rather than legal questions.

(2) Civil liberties are protected primarily by social and political pressures rather than by any activities of the courts.

(3) Many relationships between government and other entities are settled by custom, political and social pressure, and negotiation, rather than by regulation or resort to law—e.g., the government controls banking and the stock exchange by informal guidance rather than legal sanctions, and most aspects of labor relations have been outside the purview of the law until recently.

(4) The modern welfare state is ignored by the courts. Successive governments have set up administrative tribunals within departments to consider appeals of the citizen. Decisions are not usually appealable to the courts.

(5) Lawyers do not serve in positions in either Parliament or the civil service to nearly the same degree as in other democracies—e.g., the United States. The generalist character of high civil servants, the lack of temporary service by professionals as in the United States, and the fact that Parliament plays little role in drafting legislation all have meant that there was little declared need for lawyers in public life. In fact, there is a high degree of dislike of lawyers among politicians, who feel that they are too narrow to be useful in public life.

The result of all these things is that a relatively small number of the major problems of modern society find their way into the courts or into law offices and chambers. Barristers practice in chambers, but not in partnership. They have little direct contact with clients. They may not serve as working company directors or be on retainer from corporations or any other client. Solicitors work solo or in small firms primarily at conveyancing, of which they have a monopoly by law, or probate work. They have increasingly lost out to accountants as general advisers to the middle classes and businesses.

Such a legal system has very great advantages. The courts are kept out of politics and are not overloaded with social and political questions or questions of any kind. They do their business with dispatch because their functions are narrower and more conventionally "legal." Also, lawyers—particularly barristers—are specialized and expert at their roles and the judicial process benefits.

Recurrent criticisms of the system are that ordinary working-class people are not served at all by lawyers, that large segments of industry and commerce lack regular legal advice, that a system of dual representation of both solicitor and barrister for clients who must go to court is expensive and inefficient. Other, more general, criticisms are that citizens cannot bring their grievances against government into the courts because judges have been reluctant to review the findings of government administrative tribunals. It is increasingly suggested that, in an era of civil rights questions, race relations controversies, and the welfare state, citizens should have more legal protection from government.

Two kinds of reforms are most often suggested. First, it is suggested that the profession itself be restructured to break down the barrier between solicitor and barrister and to permit specialists of various kinds to practice in firms together. It is suggested that this would permit a greater division of labor among lawyers and allow them to advise a greater variety of clients. Second, it is recommended that ways be found to involve the courts more in the affairs of government, so that citizens may have protection. Some reformers have even advocated a written constitution, so that "constitutional" cases can be created.

Of the six barristers, four had been parliamentary candidates, two from each major party. Their legal practices were quite diverse, ranging from planning law to libel questions to corporate litigation. Of the five solicitors, one was a teacher of law, another a labor lawyer who also worked for a government body charged with implementing race relations legislation, another was a teacher and advocate of planning law reform, and two were in conventional business and family practice.

The most innovative of the lot was the academic. He is the foremost advocate of reform of the profession in England. He has studied law in the United States and practiced in an American firm. In England, he has been both barrister and solicitor. His mission in life is to reform the profession; he says of his American experience:

> First of all, it's given me a number of ideas—specific, concrete ideas—of things that need to be done here: improvement in legal education, improvements in the organization of [the] legal profession.
>
> I really think what America did for me was to light the fuse. I mean, the material was all there and I had a sort of general feeling of dissatisfaction about England. . . . I hadn't really quite decided what to do or how to do it and what side of the profession to practice on . . . and all those things took shape in America. . . . When I came back from America I knew what I wanted to do in general terms—I

wanted to reform the English legal profession—I wanted to reform English legal education: two modest little aims.

He has three goals: (1) to merge the two branches of the profession, (2) to develop new legal services for the poor and working classes, and (3) to shape legal education along American lines, with much more integration of law and social science. His personal role model is that of the American law school professor who moves through a number of institutional worlds and he would like to see English lawyers with greater mobility:

> I think that the rigidity of structure, whether you are either a lawyer in private practice, or you are a civil servant, or you are a politician—there is virtually no coming and going—is a great impoverishment as compared to the American system, where you learn two or three years in private practice, then you go into government for a few years, then you go back to private practice and then maybe you teach for five years, then you go into business as a lawyer. I don't guess it is particularly easy, but the whole concept of moving on and doing different things in your lifetime seems to me to be very sensible.

While the American legal profession was his ideal—"the closer we get to the American model, the better"—he understands that reform cannot just copy America:

> It's got to be fitted into the English context but more than that . . . as many as possible of its American connotations have got to be dismantled and hidden away. We are just in sight of producing a report on law firms, recommending the reintroduction of neighborhood law firms. . . . And in my original draft of the report it was put on the basis that these work very well in America and therefore with modifications would work here. The Committee didn't like that at all.
>
> Certainly you don't say—this is what they have got abroad and we ought to import it. The response to that is that it may work very well abroad but we are not abroad—we're English. The English are, in fact, quite prepared to ignore evidence that is on any view acceptable. . . . And results achieved abroad mean nothing at all.

His belief in merger of the solicitors and barristers into one profession is based on the assumption that clients would be better served. He wants a more adversary process:

> There is in the Bar an objectivity and detachment which is valuable . . . in the divided profession the barrister becomes a kind of junior judge, for pretrial settlement, for example. A client who gets

outraged about something goes to his solicitor . . . and the solicitor says, "Quite right . . . we'll sue." And then he instructs a barrister to sue and the barrister looks at it and says, "Well, I really don't fancy your chances here"—this sort of approach, soothing the client down. . . . Well, that's a valuable function and the barrister is better able to perform it than in a unified profession merely because of the distance and the fact that the remoteness creates its own atmosphere.

But I think also the objectivity and detachment has this reverse side, that lack of involvement to some extent affects performance, at least in terms of the final ounce of energy. . . . If you don't really care what the result is, if you are not particularly concerned about the client's fate, and you don't have to explain to him what it was that went wrong, there is a slight danger that you might not take quite so much trouble as you might otherwise have done.

This is a call for the barrister to become less of an officer of the court and more of an advocate for his client. It is in line with the general desire to get lawyers more involved with all kinds of "clients" in the society and out of their sheltered cloisters. Three of the barristers supported merger, but three did not, and one joined the issue well:

I can see the force of it. Big business would like to have access frequently to something more like an American law firm. . . . Our being a separate branch has the enormous advantage of total independence. The fact that we don't get our living from anyone in particular is a valuable thing. I've acted for some corporations time and time again, but not all that often. I'm not their tame lawyer. Any member of the Bar doesn't give a bugger whether what he says pleases the client or not. In the long run, one is going to do much better by saying what is right, whether either the solicitor or the client likes it or not.

This is an old attitude of "corporativism" which is reinforced by the physical atmosphere and social system of the Inns of Court. It is the very atmosphere which our reformer is trying to break up. However, his critics suggest that the price to be paid in loss of autonomy for the members of the Bar is too great. They might become tame lawyers.

However, the majority of the lawyers felt that merger was desirable on the whole. It would break lawyers out of their cocoons.

A second argument, made in extreme form by the academic reformer, is that in behalf of a written constitution:

It would be a means of developing an approach to a particular series of problems . . . at the moment, there isn't anything to get hold of.

For example, the police don't allow you to speak to a solicitor and you pull out your copy of the judges' rules and you say it says here in rule 14 that a suspect under interrogation by the police must be allowed to speak to a solicitor. . . . The policeman may then say, "Well, you know, sir, that goes on to add provided this doesn't interfere with the principle of justice." And you say, "Well, whatever that means, I want to speak to my solicitor" and subsequently you raise it in court as a matter relative to the fact that you've made a statement on something which is damaging, which you wouldn't have made if you had been properly advised. . . . There's no way of getting that complaint on its feet, really, without a constitution.

There was little interest in this idea among the others. But five seemed to share the spirit that the law be made more "constitutional." Two of these were also "Americans" in their ideas. Both have studied and practiced in the United States, and one was active in the civil rights movement. They are among the principal inspirers of the reform race relations legislation passed by the Labour government. As one said of the two of them: "We regard ourselves as the civil rights profession in this country." The first, a barrister, said of his American experience, "I don't think I'd have practiced if I hadn't been in the states. . . . I saw what a lawyer could do in society. I'm very political with a small p. Law is a vehicle for this."

He described his race relations work:

You've got to get powers for yourself, weapons. We started out with none. . . . When I came back from the United States, I was teaching in a night school. I couldn't get jobs for the colored students. It became pretty clear that one had to get a law. Our one success in 1964 was to get a Race Relations Board. It created a vested lobby. . . . I'm really concerned about the equal opportunity part. I've never regarded harmony per se as that good, and this is why I'm not a white liberal. I focus on rights. If you guarantee rights and change people's status in society so that black people have good jobs. . . . In that sense, I'm a typical American lawyer.

He advocated a much broader system of administrative law in which citizens could appeal government administrative actions to the courts:

The fact that you have document guaranteeing rights is a useful political weapon and can be a useful legal weapon. We have got to adapt our institutions. We should not dilute the executive but set up countervailing forces.

The second, a solicitor, sees himself in a freewheeling political role as a lawyer: "I tend to get involved with semi-political sorts of legal questions to do with race relations. . . . I've been responsible for the only two serious attempts to get the courts to intervene in the system of immigration control."

And later:

> What he [the English lawyer] ought to have, which most lawyers don't, is a creative attitude to the law. The American attitude lends itself to this. With a written constitution—in the United States you can go to court on a constitutional provision. There's room for the judges to deal with an issue not bound by precedent. There is more room for this in English law than some might think.

Lest we think this attitude toward using law as a political vehicle is only for those on the Left, we look at a barrister who is a Conservative Parliamentary candidate who regards himself as a "radical" in his desire to make English society more economically competitive and more productive. He favors the formation of "legal supermarkets," firms of many partners, with wide division of labor to serve many different clients. He had recently won a case against a ministry, acting for parents opposing a directive that a grammar school be made "comprehensive." The court ruled that the minister had not followed proper procedures:

> I am fascinated by using the opportunity of cases to challenge the existing legal structure. . . . I think you can in fact get some changes through more quickly and more dramatically than I think you can politically.

> I'm actually advising on passports at the moment, on the withdrawal of passports. And I think, in fact, we've got a fair run to break open the executive's power on that. But it's required a lot of looking, not only at American law but at areas of law in this country which are far removed from it in order to find a principle on which the judges can hang an essentially liberal hat.

The ideas of these legal reformers, whether they are on the political Left or the Right, seem to favor using law to protect the individual citizen against authority. And for this to be done by lawyers requires the courts to extend their willingness to consider actions of government.

Two others, a barrister and a solicitor, are active in race relations and planning law, respectively, in much the same ways as those described. Another barrister is a Conservative Parliamentary candidate who pours his innovative energies into politics. He is skeptical about lawyers playing broader roles in the society, especially in government as "in and outers" like their American counterparts. He spent a year at Yale Law School:

I found it such a remarkable place and interesting institution that it warned me of the dangers of the narrow legalistic approach.

Lawyers in America have a much wider role. English lawyers would be unqualified to do what the American lawyers do. I would oppose the extension of lawyers' powers on the basis that they are not qualified to exercise them because of their training. English lawyers as "in and outers" might be appalling unless you change English legal education.

All eleven felt this way about English lawyers serving temporarily in government. They were ill-prepared for it. Reform of the profession should come first.

Four of the group, two barristers and two solicitors, were in general sympathetic with the ideas expressed by the others, but none of them was particularly playing "innovative" roles in his work. They seemed content in each case to do their work well within accepted paths. Unlike the others, these four were not particularly under the influence of American experience or models.

These reformers are perhaps too much under the influence of American ideas. They are not sure about how to adapt these models to English practice. History may have passed them by, in the sense that it is too late to extend the role of law and the lawyer in English social life. However, new kinds of law are developing: race relations, industrial disputes, and administrative law. Government itself may pull the lawyer more into political spheres, thus making new roles for lawyers.

American models of legal practice are particularly appealing to these English innovators because they provide exactly what is seen to be lacking in Britain. In the United States, one finds wide-ranging social roles for lawyers which have existed since colonial times. American lawyers very early broke down the European distinctions between types of legal practice, and the lawyer in a frontier society became the all-purpose generalist in matters of conflict. One also finds a close relationship between law and politics in large part because constitutional questions are, in fact, political questions, given the need for interpretation of a written constitution. And, finally, like the other professions in America, and unlike England, law is an academic profession which is closely linked to professional school within the universities. This gives law and the other professions a tie to scholarship which is missing in the English practical apprenticeship system. Theory and practice serve each other in American law.

Parsons (1968) has posited that

the new legal profession, with the strong involvement of its academic branch, has become the most important professional agency for implementing the moral consensus (incomplete as it is) of American society, in the first instance, but more broadly of modern society in general. The crucial focus, perhaps, is on the concept of right, which controls the area in which moral claims, in one of the most important spheres of interpenetration in all of social structures, fuse with governmental and other social obligations.

These English reformers want what American lawyers have. They see a need for wider social roles for lawyers in English society, whether it be serving the needs of modern sectors of business or providing for lawyers for the poor. They also see a need for a new constitutional approach with regard to new kinds of questions in which it is felt the citizen lacks adequate protection, such as race, administrative law, and the welfare bureaucracy. The logic of social change here is that of change from status to contract relationships in the relation of citizen to government. There is a decline of deference for generalist governmental elites, and their discretionary powers and a greater concern that citizens be protected against bureaucracy by specific kinds of principles which can be invoked constitutionally in law. And, in light of this desire for wider roles, there is an interest in more academic training for lawyers in professional law schools which would link the profession to academic knowledge and thus give it capabilities for growth and change now lacking in the apprenticeship educational system which prepares lawyers for traditional roles.

The same pattern of innovation is seen in both planners and lawyers. Replace elitist generalists with client-oriented specialists and increase the variety of social roles open to the profession so that it will work in a more adversary way for clients in situations of greater pluralist conflict, but also greater protection for the client. A certain loss of hierarchy and community is to be compensated for by a gain in individuality.

## SOCIAL SCIENTISTS

### Economists

There is little place for the "in and outer" in Whitehall, because the top advisers to ministers are permanent civil servants. It is here that the charge of "amateurism" has been most shrill. There have been economists in the specialist grades of the civil service, but they have been civil servants in subordinate positions and not academics. The Treasury, the chief economic unit of British government, has gotten along without academic visitors most of the time. The Labour government of 1964-1969 brought in a small number of academic economists as advisers to ministers in order to demonstrate its intention to galvanize economic policies in the direction of growth. The count varies from time to time, but there were anywhere from eight to ten such people serving at any given time, most of them young.

Of the seven interviewed, three were "in" at that time, one had been in and was hoping to return with a Conservative government, another was a former civil servant in the Treasury, and two were regular consultants to ministries. Two were personal advisers to ministers, and two were advisers to party leaders.

All embraced the desirability of the in and outer role, not only for themselves, but for professionals in general. The former civil servant summed up a general feeling about the civil service:

> One of the weaknesses of the civil service has always been that the whole training and position, etc. . . . is geared to producing Permanent Secretaries. The trouble is that only 25 out of 2,000 are Permanent Secretaries at any one time. An economist who has worked in Whitehall, in international organizations, in journalism, has a much wider range of experience to be in charge of a government department. . . . I don't think there's any virtue in being a so-called "generalist." Generalist is just a polite way of saying that somebody knows nothing.

> I enormously admire Washington in the sense that you have the ability to say, "Look, you want to do this job and we want to get that guy and we'll get him to do it, whether he's at RAND or Harvard or Ford or General Motors."

An adviser to a minister presents a picture of the need for economists in Whitehall and the skills they bring:

> Well, taking the ideal economist, the sort of thing he ought to bring in is a desire for numbers the whole time; never decide issues as being substantially [this] or overwhelmingly that or clearly something or other. . . . The administrative civil servant is much more concerned with logical categories which he can defend in Parliament.

> The second thing is a feeling for the marginal which goes with numbers, a little bit more, a little bit less, elasticity concepts, marginal revenue concepts . . . you know, one looks at issues like getting out of _____ , which we've just ditched. Well, I was on committees on this in 1965 and most of the ideas which were put up were things like, "It'll go down very badly with our European partners"—of course, however worse if we give it up later? How much more would we have to put in? . . . These are the things that I think are absolutely crucial.

They [ministers] must come in knowing what they want to do: what they don't know is how to do it. What they must bring in with them, I think, is their own chaps, who know how to do it, and what I want, therefore, is incoming ministers to have their "cabinets" as the French do . . . chaps who are sympathetic and who go when he goes . . . who have no future career in the civil service. They are his servants just as I am _____'s servant here. When he resigns. . . . I don't think I'll last a day and I don't want to. . . . Now the civil servant can't do that because they serve a whole series of masters. . . . The minister is then defended . . . he then has support. He has an equal source of power vis-à-vis those who don't want to do anything particularly.

Civil servants are seen as inhospitable to new ideas. As one put it:

Oh, it's control over options, really. . . . Over the alternatives presented to ministers. Minister wants to do such as having cheap housing finance. . . . Well, there it is, "It can't be done, minister. I'm sorry, but there are all the reasons why." Now, some ministers will say, "It's going to be done, you just tell me how to do it."

But there are others who say, "Oh, well then, what can we do?" "Well, now as it heppens we have a file here," and then you can see that the minister is tremendously impressed that they've thought of everything. The reason why they've thought of everything is that they've looked at all these problems twenty times over, and they've got the line, the departmental line.

If a new minister wants to look at it, then of course he's omnipotent . . . but he can't be as omnipotent as that every day on every issue with all his underlings and be a member of the Cabinet and appear at the House and go back to his constituents. It wears anybody out. So naturally, the chaps who are there for a career, the long-haul guys, they win.

The conclusion that is drawn by these experts is that ministers need help from people like them in order to be able to think of new ways to innovate and in order to be able to evaluate proposals from civil servants. A former adviser in an economic ministry said:

The civil servants who advised on the decision [to curtail imports] — no one ever made an effort to estimate the effect. The committee did not include a single person competent to make such an estimate or even who thought of making such an estimate. And the first point of doing this is to say, what effect is it having? And the papers of this committee happened to come through us by mistake. We pounced on them and shook that committee up.

One who is adviser to an economic minister gives a picture of working to justify one's role with civil servants:

> They [civil servants] hate having their toes trodden on by temporaries. They don't mind the professional, established, civil service economic advisers, because they do technical jobs. They object to chaps like me sort of wallowing around and making a nuisance of themselves.
>
> But, since devaluation, this has changed a bit because there is such a host of most ghastly problems confronting us every week that one goes through fire together and one gets welded. . . . There are still tensions and all that, but a bit of mutual respect goes up because they see that at a pinch you can be sent away to do a useful job of work for an hour or two and produce a draft paper which will save them some work.
>
> It depends enormously upon being prepared to make a go of it. If we got half our colleagues from the universities who were economists and brought them in the machine, the results would be disastrous. There are very few chaps who can make a go of this. . . . I mean academics are academics, and administrative is administrative. But there are some of us who are prepared to fill in, and perhaps they should do the job.

It is clear that none of these people feel that their role as "in and outer" had been institutionalized to any degree at all. They are alone in an unfriendly environment and must work to build up legitimacy for themselves from civil servants.

We get glimpses of a constructive compromise in which each group teaches the other. We have already seen how they think they teach civil servants. Here are two reports of how they learn from civil servants; first from the adviser cited above:

> He [civil servant] shows one how to operate. It's fun to learn how to operate. It's like learning how to sail a boat . . . which rope to pull at which time to get which result. It's also more than that. In particular fields, they have an enormous amount of experience and knowledge and one can get one's corners rubbed off more usefully.

And another who has been in twice:

> I'm a bit skeptical about whether a man who doesn't really know Whitehall can suddenly get charge and operate a bit of it. Somebody could come in from outside if he had already been in at a junior level and knew the way the system works. But for somebody accustomed to a different system, which may be more or less hierarchical, where

you don't have responsibility to ministers and have a different division of labor . . . is . . . rather difficult.

A lot of advice to the minister will be semi-political, keeping his own end up in Cabinet, etc. . . . And you need background and experience in Cabinet politics.

In this job, the fact that I've had two years in the civil service has been extremely valuable. I know those chaps in Whitehall and can ring them up. It's quite important. Without it, I'd be less effective.

I think a lot of people feel that when Kennedy came in with a lot of new chaps, a lot of new ideas got seriously considered. And when the outsiders came into Whitehall with the Labour government, they just got bogged down in the marsh, and the administrative class won. This is true to some extent, but some of the people who came in were naive about what was politically and administratively possible. They were probably more naive than Americans, who are much better informed about government.

These interviews were completed before the Fulton report was released in June 1968, but their ideas anticipated many of the leading conclusions and recommendations of the report, in particular the criticism of generalist civil servants and the recommendation of greater mobility of a variety of professionals in and out of bureaucracy. The Fulton report shared the same reform ethos as these economists. However, it seems clear that goals desired can be achieved only by the implementation of Fulton by governments. Individual academics, serving as in and outers, can do little to change the subculture of British bureaucracy.

## Political Scientists

All of but two of the group feel that political scientists have a useful contribution to make in government advisory roles, but even the positive views are constrained by the fact that their advice is so close to that which is characteristic of the political leader himself. The chairman of a department in a new university is the most hopeful. He consults regularly with a ministry and bases his views on personal experience:

just the same as the economist, only from a professional point of view. I mean this is the absurd thing, that the economists for various historical reasons have established their unique capacity to analyze things in ways that will be useful to policy makers, but other social sciences haven't, and the results are plain for all to see . . . with predictably unsatisfactory results. You see this very clearly in the case of development planning, which could almost become an economist's prerogative exclusively, but you also see it in any policy decisions involving variables which sociologists aren't competent to analyze with the notion that everything else is the business of the general administrator and his technical advisers, and very often these don't exist or aren't very professional or don't really consider what has to be looked at. I mean the British "plan" in a way, although it was knocked for six, partly by environmental changes that weren't foreseen; these were forseeable by some people, to some extent, and any plan for the British economy with its enormous, largely undirected private sector will depend primarily on the skill with which such instruments as the government has at its disposal are exercised to change cultural and social structural variables. Who is to do this work? ... It's our fault to a large extent this hasn't happened.

A lecturer at another new university amplifies this view:

Economists tend to say "other things being equal," or something, and accept political problems and balance of political forces as something extraneous to a system and something you try to eliminate, rather than see as part of the system.

There ought to be some way for people to say, "Yes, that's all very well, but it won't work" or "You'll get it done twice as quickly if you ask among the representatives of such and such a pressure group."

As one put it, political scientists could give advice to increase the "political literacy" of civil servants.

Two were less optimistic. One point of view was expressed by a Labour Party supporter of working-class background who has very traditional ideas about British governmental institutions:

I'd be useless. I would want to go in for what I could get out to improve my capacities as a political scientist. I'm sure they [ministers and administrative class civil servants] know more about the working of the machine than I do. It would be very arrogant of me to think I would have something to contribute. . . . I see no lack of awareness and use of social science by government. The problem is what use of it is made by the Cabinet in decision-making.

However, all shared the common view that the chief contribution of political scientists was as a general force for education about politics and governmental processes.

As one argues:

I don't think he [political scientist] makes the process of governing more scientific. I think he creates an understanding of what is

involved in governing, which should help people understand what politics is about, and what the activities of a politician involve, and what democracy involves. . . . It doesn't impinge directly on governors, but more on the governed. . . . It can improve the quality of government, if only because it can improve the communication.

A department chairman at a redbrick university, who has been a leader in the effort at Parliamentary reform through his writing and direct personal lobbying with members of Parliament, expresses the philosophy of government which underlies his views about Parliamentary reform and, in so doing, illustrates the educative function of the political scientist:

> One could put forward a model . . . that an autocracy might have been able to have traditionally a fairly effective internal communication system amongst the large enough body of men who need to govern it and still small enough to keep a very informal communication system . . . but mobilization regimes have got to reach beyond this, and I think it's after the approach of the industrial revolution: you get the discovery of propaganda, but somehow propaganda is seen as something quite apart from accurately finding out. . . . Well, firstly the census . . . then you begin to get rather crude measures of what they want, of which the vote is probably the most relevant— the Gallup Polls. . . . But then everybody's wanting some third kind of measure that partly rises out of political experience and partly, I suppose, could be supplemented by superior kinds of surveys.

> I mean, as an example, the British prices and incomes policy, when it was launched, was a declaration of intent that both sides would do their jolly best for fair wages and prices. But nobody made the slightest effort to find out whether on the shop floor (a) people were likely to understand it, or (b) whether they were likely to stand for it. Any government must become more involved in this kind of activity, not necessarily to tie its hands, but it may be partially instrumental when they want to know what the odds are. . . . They shouldn't go into it by guess or by God or by political hunch quite as much as they have done.

Here is the political scientist working from his understanding of the dynamics of government, acting as publicist and reformer to call upon government to do things in new ways.

The general impression one gets from listening to these people is that they see the chief role of political scientists in the current period of reform as not being to work in government, but to be educators in the society about the need to change government and governing in various ways. They are agents of change in the political culture, especially among the elite who are their students.

## Managers

During the interviews, they gave the impression of coiled springs ready to break loose. One got a sense of visceral energy. They are crusaders of a kind, very much modernizers in their own eyes, who see themselves as bringing the skills and drives of modern management to a society that desperately needs greater productivity and profit.

Eight worked as executives with large corporations, most of international scope. Three were currently working in government, one at the Prices and Incomes Board and two in the Industrial Reconstruction Corporation. One was a vice chairman of a national political party executive. Another had been a Conservative Parliamentary candidate.

Eight were explicitly critical of what they took to be traditional English styles of management. As the manager of exports for a corporation put it:

> I am interested to look at the difference between the American in business and his counterpart in England. . . . The basic difference is that most of the American managers are anxious, very anxiously looking at the prospects of making considerably more money next year than this so he can buy a bigger car or "Let's join the country club." But there are so many people in this country in middle management, secure business conditions, who have their little house, their little car, and what they really want is to have people go away and leave them alone.

Or another man in comparable position:

> thinking of the run of the mill engineering firm in the Midlands—the last thing they want is brains. They want experience, and that's all. Industry, particularly middling industry in this country, has been too long governed by experienced people—and at the very top, financial brains. Brains in commerce and industry have gone much more to finance than to operating management.

> There is a terrible distrust of intellectualism in this country. You often hear people referred to—"He's a very bright chap, but he's awfully nice," which is pathetic. In Germany, people would say, "He's very intelligent, which makes him nice."

The older generation of managers was characterized as addicted to muddling through, to lacking innovativeness and acquisitive drives. Stability has been preferred to achievement, with consequences in slow economic growth.

Therefore, new styles were needed in management. The emphasis here was upon learned techniques, particularly imitating American models. One wonders if this is not a bit imitative and wooden. A recent graduate of the

London postgraduate business school describes the kinds of management patterns generally cited as needed:

> One of the things that intrigues me is the work I have been involved in, in trying to introduce and bring about change in the operations of the company, the process of integration and the development of systems. This is something we lack rather badly—control systems of all kinds.
>
> I have a unique advantage of being able to look at our American counterparts at fairly regular intervals. Superficially, they look—on the selling side—to outsiders like a high three-ring circus, with lots of fellows with big motorcars and expense accounts appearing to have all sorts of flexibility within their command. If you look beneath the surface, the whole corporation is motivated and controlled by pretty specific control mechanisms. The salesmen and plant have their targets and are required to forecast. It's this control mechanism that enables people at the top to run the company.
>
> In this company, there has been far too great a tendency to engage in general debate about the company problem and too little evidence of a willingness to get down and tackle specific problems objectively. There's quite a rift between the, if you like, Oxford Union type of debate—and the level and standard of this debate is very high indeed . . . at the other end of the scale, you have got people wishing to deal with a very short-term problem, something that can be solved today or in a few days. But nothing in the intermediate area, which sets targets which are aimed at achieving certain specific results and constructing a program.

The significance of these remarks is that we see a search for a new kind of managerial skill, based upon American models, which will link generalists at the top and specialists at the base in concerted control and planning mechanisms and which will broaden, and yet sharpen, the understanding of each. This is precisely the managerial skill which the Fulton report on the civil service called for in the higher civil service. The quotation illustrates the congruence of ideas about managerial styles in private and public spheres. New styles are developing simultaneously in both areas.

Every one of them feels that more businessmen of a modern cast of mind are needed in politics and government. A marketing manager for a large chemical company expresses the common view:

> Parliament has got the wrong people in it . . . not the sort of people who can understand and tackle economic problems. The people best able to do this are all working for organizations such as Unilever and Shell and ICI. . . . Businessmen in Parliament on the Tory side tend

to have money and family traditions of Parliamentary service, and doubtless they are quite admirable in many ways—and in many cases they are people who almost by definition want to maintain the status quo. On the Labour side, you tend to get teachers, doctors, journalists, lawyers as well, and almost by definition with the kinds of jobs they've got, it seems unlikely to me that they can handle the sort of problems which we face, which are essentially ones of definition and organization.

The majority of the managers had not served in government and therefore their ideas about such service were much closer to stereotypes than those of other professionals. A theme of ambivalence came up in most of the responses. On the one hand, businessmen could bring much-needed order and method and drive to government. On the other hand, a skepticism was expressed that public bureaucracy could really be structured, in its red tape and sluggishness, to give full scope to the driving energies with which they saw themselves blessed.

The Labour government of 1964 brought a number of businessmen into Whitehall. They were given operational tasks in the Department of Economic Affairs, the Prices and Incomes Board, the Ministry of Technology, the Industrial Reconstruction Corporation and the National Economic Development Corporation. They tended to be young and to know how to use techniques and methodologies which the older generation of managers simply does not have.

The managers saw themselves as bringing the qualities of drive for accomplishment and organizational skill to Whitehall.

Here are some characteristic comments. The first is from a Harvard-trained merchant banker temporarily working in one of the new agencies: "Businessmen bring drive to government, something a civil servant is not trained to do. But businessmen are narrow and single-purposed."

Next, from a marketing executive who is a national officer of the Liberal Party and a Parliamentary candidate:

I think it would be very good to have one or two less cautious, less balanced and more thrustful people, you know, grit in the oyster argument. . . . The good manager is achievement-oriented. He also may be extraordinarily limited in outlook. Their success rests on having been blinkered.

An advertising executive, who had been a Tory candidate, said:

Secondment is good. The government learns to respect the problems business has to face. The manager in government, in theory, is acutely concerned with commercial return. The academic will be

concerned at the grand design. The civil servant will be interested in
ministerial goals and departmental efficiency. The industrial man
could be successful at widening problems—for example, in overseas
relations, go beyond the Board of Trade perspective. The civil service
is dreadfully overdepartmentalized. Academics couldn't help to solve
that—to force a coalition of action. But the commercial man
recognizes that decisions must have a rippling effect. He is
accustomed to seeing market forces.

Three of these eleven people had actually worked in Whitehall, but
their characterizations of the manager's role and skills were the same as the
uninitiated.

The difficulties of the businessman adapting to government were
described by one of the informants, an economic journalist with Whitehall
experience:

From my experience, the businessman would say, "Here is the
problem, the obvious solution is x, y, z." The civil servant would
say, "Have you thought of a, b, c?" The businessman hadn't, so he
loses every time. The habits of decision of the manager are to be
creative in the big things, and the pennies don't matter. But civil
servants are trained to look at all the facets of a thing. So some
businessmen never learned how to work well in the governmental
system. And, in a given decision, the businessman may be right.

The experience of managers in Whitehall does not seem much different
from that of the economists. They have difficulty adapting to the styles of
civil servants and tend to stay the grit in the oyster. This suggests that
mere secondment of individuals into the bosom of Whitehall is not
sufficient to change styles of administration. An investment consultant,
now temporarily a civil servant, describes his actual feeling of being at sea
in Whitehall. He is responding to the question of what skills a good
businessman brings to government:

Oh, I think knowledge of finance is the most important thing. I'm
still amazed how ignorant these people who I have come in contact
with are of financial principles and particularly the pure administrators, civil servants. Possibly, a willingness to be slightly more
independent in their way of thinking . . . I haven't been there long
enough to know how it's going to react on me personally. To begin
with, I know I felt slightly frightened that anything I might say
might create a protest meeting of tenants in Walsall, that did frighten
me, as I am only used to a very small and specialized firm in a way. I
think I'm getting used to that now. I've been completely sort of
quiet. How it will turn out a bit later on, I really don't know.

The most striking comments of all were in strong criticisms of the element of ascription in the class system and selection of elites and in what has loosely been called the establishment. All expressed such views, and one sees that they are rooted in their very life styles. They are crusaders against the slothful habits of the past, which they identify with the establishment. However, one also sees that the transition has been painful for some, probably especially so for people of this generation who were reared with establishment expectations and have now turned against them.

A merchant banker, now working in Whitehall, describes the great impact that the Harvard Business School had on him:

> I read English literature at Oxford. My education was very narrow, no math or science. I deliberately went to Harvard to compensate. Wanted to be a businessman because England needs them. Harvard Business School and the United States were eye openers. I saw and admired American problem-solving and particularly American social equality. I noticed that there was none of the public school-grammar school split which so constrains, even at Oxford. I still feel constrained—cannot talk comfortably to a British working man.

The advertising executive indicates the change in occupational goals that has occurred in his time:

> Industry is now a far greater employer of the nation's talent than ten years ago. Then, it was the Foreign Office. Now, only a stupid ass will go in the Foreign Office. We used to talk about the Bar or even the civil service. Now people are ready for industry.

An oil executive, Oxford-educated, an officer in the army but of working-class background, describes an ideal for a future elite:

> I would like it to be a functional meritocracy, as opposed to a class aristocracy. What I would like to feel is that a top man in the law or business does not necessarily feel that he has more in common with a top man in politics or the arts. I would rather like him to feel that he has more in common with the top man in his own field. . . . This is the sort of tension which has got to replace the current motivating force, which is basically class consciousness.

The managers are the most Benthamite of any of the four occupational groups, the most eager to rationalize folkways and institutions, and the least inclined to wish to balance the traditional and the new.

CONCLUSION

These Englishmen have linked innovativeness in professional roles with the general Benthamite revolution at work in the society. Old institutions are to be infused with new roles and a new utilitarian spirit. We see the following ideas in common among these different professionals:

(1) criticism of diffuse elite roles of generalized authority, whether it be in planning, law, or bureaucracy, and advocacy of greater specificity of expertise and roles among elites;

(2) desire for increased professional mobility across institutional boundaries;

(3) admiration for American models of the relations of the professions to government, because such models would seem to supply the cross-fertilization of professional styles which British institutions are seen to need;

(4) borrowing of techniques and methods of practice from American professions, which are seen as more developed in the utilization of knowledge in professional tasks, but concern to fuse such new knowledge with traditional normative goals of English professions;

(5) sense of incompleteness as innovators; realization that creation of new professional roles cannot be fulfilled without the support and cooperation of other elites and without role changes in other elites;

(6) desire to increase the capabilities of established institutions, rather than to weaken them through the infusion of new professional roles.

## CHAPTER IV
## A THEORY OF PROFESSIONALS AND INNOVATION

We have found a congruence of thought in ideas about society, government, and professions and have labeled this broad ideology Benthamite. The historical analogy is with the utilitarians of the nineteenth century, who rationalized a number of English institutions and social practices in reaction against traditional hierarchies and elite values. The utilitarians were counter-elites, who were eventually comfortably amalgamated with traditional elites. The same process is at work today.

Why do these individuals share this Benthamite ideology? They were deliberately selected because they were thought to be innovative in terms of the general spirit of social criticism. But we lack a control group for comparison. We may be looking at a microcosm of a generation. But these individuals may share certain characteristics in greater degree and intensity than other members of their generation, although there are clearly many young professionals like our subjects in the society.

In Chapter II, we saw that characteristics of social background could explain a social "radicalism" in the case of some, but not all, of the subjects. A number of other complementary partial explanations of ideology can be suggested. They are youngish and think in future-oriented terms. They are ambitiously making their careers and identify with what they see to be progressive trends in the society. Only a handful of them can be said to be genuinely creative in an inventive sense. Most are innovative in that they seek to apply ideas derived from elsewhere. Inventiveness can be seen in people like the legal reformer or the systems planner, but even those who are developing new professional roles, such as the economists in government, are acting on a stage prepared by others.

If social background and age are factors to predispose them to be innovative, what can we attribute to profession? They are to some extent "outsiders" vis-à-vis official "establishments" in their professions. Planners are very much subordinate to politicians and civil servants in Whitehall, as are academic social scientists and managers working as temporaries. The dominant ethos of older generations within each of these professions is antithetical to the styles of these younger men. The young planners are in revolt against elitist and architectural approaches. The innovative lawyers wish to shake the profession out of its comfortable cocoons. Social scientists bring a greater methodological sophistication and are critical of the tradition of empiricism in social research which is too often impressionistic. Young managers protest the amateurism and slipshod character of British management.

The cognitive styles of the younger generation are much more scientific, quantitative, and rationalistic than the norm in their fields. This is, of course, less true of the law, which is not a scientific discipline. But even here, there were strong pleas for legal education to be more closely tied to the social sciences. These young elites reflect the slow breaking down of the walls of separation between profession and university and academic life in Britain. They affirm their professions as properly linked to changing and growing bodies of academic knowledge and reject the practical apprenticeship system of training. This cognitive style, therefore, makes them critical of what they perceive to be an overreliance on generalist, intuitive methods of problem analysis and solution in establishments.

Each of these factors helps explain the total picture, but none is sufficient by itself to do so. Their social backgrounds predispose them to be "radicals," as does their youth. They stand outside "establishments" and are convinced that they are better educated and more skilled than those within. Some are genuinely creative at social invention and respond to this factor in personality. Most have simply embraced the dominant reform ideology of the times. But they do so because of all the predisposing factors.

The most salient conflict of values among elites in England in the sixties was between traditionalists and utilitarians, whether on Right or Left. Our subjects could not help but be caught up on the side of reform. We have seen clusters of social and institutional characteristics poised for battle in their thinking. Hierarchy, secrecy, elitism, amateurism, and unscientific impressionism are arrayed against openness, decentralization, the principle of participation, and specialization and scientific rationalism. And American models, which seem to embody the traits of the latter cluster, are invoked as the basis for reform. The internal logic of the two clusters is not great. Openness and expertise do not necessarily go together except insofar as one is critical of the combination of secrecy and amateurism. An elite is being criticized by a counter-elite which would like to replace it, or at least get it to move over a little.

All the personality and background factors are focused and strengthened by professional position in the society and the professional commitment to innovative cognitive styles. The call for new professional roles in the society follows from these factors. We thus explain the adherence to the Benthamite ideology by the tension between their personal professional norms and values and what they take to be the prevailing norms and values in their fields and in the elite levels of society and government.

An adaptation of the Parsonian model of a stable but changing social system is helpful in describing the role of professionals as innovators in contemporary Britain. A stable system is integrated from the top down by dominant values and norms. There is a congruence of values in many different social spheres. Institutions reflect these values and norms and are embedded with roles which will implement them. Roles in an integrated social system thus make for pattern maintenance (Mitchell, 1967).

However, roles can be a source of innovation in institutions, values, and norms. Role change serves the function of adaptation of the society to new tasks. We will define "modernization" in advanced industrial societies as the continuous development and application of knowledge to social life. Roles can then be the key to modernization and adaptation insofar as they are linked to new knowledge and promote the dissemination and application of such knowledge. Roles of this kind thus feel a strain between old values and norms and accepted modes of thought and new tasks for social institutions. And this strain, when combined with knowledge capabilities, is the source of innovation.

The professions are at the cutting edge of role change of this kind if they are actively linked to sources of new knowledge. Innovative professionals are brokers between the dominant values and norms of a culture, including prevailing modes of thought, and new knowledge and new functional imperatives for the society requiring the application of new knowledge. They have the task of adapting the dominant values, norms, and modes of thought to new tasks and overcoming the existence of strain.

The majority of professionals will be well insulated within protective professional systems and may resist new roles and even new knowledge. The innovators are likely to come from a gradually emerging counter-elite which seeks to create new professional roles. They are people who are more sensitive to the existence of strain and more anxious to be inventive and innovative. They are likely to be young, to be the best educated people in their disciplines, to be highly specialized and yet cosmopolitan in their social experience, and to be somewhat marginal to the mainstream of the profession (Chandler, 1962: 314-323).

The industrial democracies would seem to be experiencing changes of this kind at present. In these societies, the function of pattern maintenance is performed by most organized professions. The bureaucratic public professions—such as the military, social workers, and permanent civil servants with professional training and skills—support established relationships between citizens and the government. The private professions—such as law, medicine, engineering, architecture, journalism, and even academia and the clergy—largely function in ways supportive of the dominant ideological ethos of liberal, capitalist society. Lawyers protect private property relationships; doctors are entrepreneurs; engineers, architects, and journalists work for managers and corporations in a capitalist system, or have such as clients. Academics and clergy for the most part accept and promote the ideologies of liberal capitalism. This is not to say that these professions cannot seek substantive social change within such parameters. But their norms and values are congruent with those of the larger society.

There are national variations of this mode. In England, one finds much guild organization of professions and strong hierarchy within professions. The links between the universities and the professions are weak. And there is a lack of horizontal mobility of professionals across institutional boundaries. There is a strong emphasis upon professional autonomy and self-regulation.

In the United States in the colonial period, there was a breaking down of specialized distinctions and hierarchy within professions—for example, that between barristers and solicitors in the law, because of the greater need and opportunity for generalist practitioners in a frontier society (Boorstin, 1968). The professions in the nineteenth century became much more fully identified with capitalist institutions than was the case in England. But they also had much stronger ties with both the universities and government. The land grant college emphasized practical professional education, but also provided for a link between research and practice. The absence of a higher civil service of elitist cast in government and the admiration for the practical man with a skill permitted professionals in both private life and civil service to be one of the chief sources of innovation within a highly permeable federal government (Price, 1954). There has been a great deal of horizontal mobility of professionals across institutions and considerable variety of role options for professionals.

This is not to say that there has not been tension between the professions and other institutions in these societies. The tension has been greater in the United States because of the lesser encapsulation of the professions than in Britain. Conservative, self-protective, professional impulses seek maximum self-regulation and resist public control. Those with a high commitment to professional conscience and autonomy chafe under the cooptation of professionals into purely instrumental roles for government and private economic power. In England, there is less entanglement of professionals with other skill and power groups and therefore less tension. Encapsulation protects professional autonomy but perhaps at the price of professional influence in the society at large.

Returning to the Parsonian model, we can see two characteristic kinds of innovation arising out of these tensions. The first is the development of new cognitive roles for professionals in response to new knowledge and social strain. The second is the assertion of professional moral wholeness and autonomy in behalf of utopian social goals and rejection of the moral alienation that comes from instrumental roles. The latter also calls for new professional roles in contrast to established ones. Such challenges come when the prevailing cognitive or normative values are under attack in the society. These challenges can be more or less reformist or radical. And there is no necessary relation between the cognitive and normative challenges. But they can be fused in a democratic credo. If that is lacking, the cognitive drive can be simply technocratic.

The English economists and managers were primarily cognitive and technocratic in their style. The American public interest lawyer of the Ralph Nader variety would be primarily normative in his style. But there are plenty of examples of a combination: English planners and lawyers; American advocacy planners and ecology activist scientists.

In general, the Englishmen of this study reveal a predominantly cognitive approach to new roles. They feel that a lack of expert brainpower has been one of the serious failings of English elite institutions. Reform is to be cognitive. Few challenge elite substantive values, but, of course, those in each of the three ideological traditions see that body of ideas as potentially dominant. There is little alienation from the goals of the society, as mediated through a tradition. One might expect a much higher proportion of young American professionals to seek new normative roles for themselves because of a reaction against the goals of liberal, capitalist society. The charge is that cognitive expertise has too often sold out at the expense of morality.

English innovators would seem to move toward American models in order to improve the quality of professional expertise and have it play a wider number of social roles. The danger is that the English professions will lose their moral autonomy and be coopted by organizational power and social ethos. One cannot have it both ways. The planners will become more political, the lawyers will be more in the market place, the social scientists will feel the tensions of governmental roles, and the managers will emphasize more acquisitive values.

## AN IDEAL TYPE

We can create an ideal type of professional as reformer by combining cognitive innovator with democratic values in a society of informational complexity. The ideal type best meets the functional imperatives of this kind of society.

The professions are among those structures in society which define the use of information in two ways: first, the technical possibility of utilizing information for the achievement of results; second, the question of whose interests are served by the results. A modern society is a functional society in the sense that social institutions must provide social functions to an increasing degree and existing institutional structures necessarily become more complex in order to fulfill these functions. New institutional patterns have to accommodate the rising flood of technological informa-tion, in the widest sense of the word, and permit the expression of a widening span of interests by an increasing number of people. Power and conflict of interest groups are not eliminated by the advent of such a functional society, but there are strong pressures to rationalize the rules by which power is distributed and give a greater equality of chances for participation in power-sharing.

Professional styles are especially conducive to the transition from a society based upon power relationships to one which, without eliminating power relationships, gives new emphasis to expanding information and participation. This is because the professions are based upon the expansion of the intellectual informational element in modern society. And they must also face the moral question of the uses of information, for what interests and to what ends?

The professional contribution is not necessarily purely amoral and technical, but carries clear implications for means and ends. Professionals are likely to carry a cybernetic commitment to openness, information-sharing, the scaling down of hierarchy, the stimulation of feedback and responsiveness in all institutions which they inhabit. They may bring a rationality to the exercise of power which will limit the arbitrary nature of power.

Innovative professionals living and working in a time of political and social development in a society are likely to evolve a critical attitude toward the status quo and seek to change the system of power as part of their professional goal. They work for equality by countering ascription by achievement norms. They keep their autonomy against the ethic of the organization. Their influence is derived from knowledge and therefore tends toward functional specialization, not overall domination. Their style is conducive to problem-solving by teams and groups of diverse professionals. Their political claim is for participation, not technocracy. The professions can best be integrated in a collaborative setting, and their social influence depends upon the general awareness of the importance of a wide sharing of information (Hage and Aiken, 1971).

Of course, this is an idealized picture of what professionals can do to effect social change and new patterns of power. One cannot deny that in the most industrialized societies the professions still carry with them past traditions of serving systems of established power and still have a strong belief in material gain as an important goal. Nor can one deny that a kind of technocratic knowledge has been lent to power holders at the same time that the professional has abdicated his moral responsibility to be concerned about the uses to which that knowledge was put.

But there is a very strong impetus in a professional ethic toward maximum sharing of information and power in modern institutions so that the functional tasks will get done (Pusic, 1969).

Organization complexity, the difficulty of delivering social and professional services and the heightened consciousness of citizens about their needs all place a great emphasis upon the precise measurement and evaluation of the effects of policies upon citizens and upon the participation of citizens in the formulation and administration of policies affecting them. One of the reasons the legislative programs of the Great Society were ineffective is that no means existed to measure effectiveness. Professionals with a cybernetic bent must devise such means. And the professional must link his traditional concern for the client with the new need for client participation (Schick, 1971). These tendencies are perhaps most highly developed in urban planning, where the master plan has given way to belief in planning as a process of continuous learning in behalf of democratic values.

Our English professionals seem so close to this ideal type because cybernetic imperatives of both cognitive and participatory kinds are part and parcel of the Benthamite revolution. Organization theory tells us that professionals within organizations seek to reduce hierarchy, increase specificity of roles, and improve learning by the organization. Seen in these terms, all English institutions are an organization, and these innovating professionals are seeking to be the grit in the oyster to open things up.

The quiet revolution of the sixties was disappointing to reformers. Parliamentary and civil service reform were limited and uncertain. Economic modernization has been very slow. However, one can safely say that the ideas of the Benthamites triumphed. The phase of attacking the establishment has been followed by the slow, dull, and unglamorous task of transforming it. This will take a generation of work in the professions, universities, business, labor, and government. However, one can hope and expect that the end result will be more effective and democratic institutions in a Britain which finds ways to combine the modern values of expertise and efficiency with the traditional humanism of concern for balance, proportion, and human scale. This is a time of creativity when the old and the new are to be once more joined.

## NOTE

1. The following sections on planners, lawyers, and economists are similar to material previously published in the *Journal of Comparative Politics,* July 1972.

## APPENDIX A. THE INFORMANTS

Planners—One faculty member of the University of London, an officer of the Town and Country Planning Association, and an officer of the Town and Country Planning Institute.

Lawyers—A planning lawyer who teaches for the Law Society, an officer of the Law Society and member of the law faculty of the London School of Economics and Political Science, and a political scientist at Strathclyde University.

Economists—Three faculty members at Oxford, Essex, and Sussex Universities.

Political Scientists—Three faculty members at Essex and York Universities and the London School of Economics and Political Science.

Managers—A faculty member of the London School of Business, a research associate of the Tavistock Institute, and a journalist for the London *Times* who writes on economics and government.

## APPENDIX B. THE SUBJECTS

### A. Social Scientists (all but two hold teaching posts)

(1) *Economist.* Teaches at a "new" university. Did graduate work in the United States. Consults regularly with a ministry.

(2) *Economist.* On leave from his university to serve as an administrator in a new government agency. Previous service in Whitehall in advisory roles.

(3) *Economist.* On leave from university to serve as economic adviser to a minister. Previous service in Whitehall in advisory roles.

(4) *Economist.* Teaches at a "new" university. Did graduate work in the United States. Adviser to a national party leader.

(5) *Economist.* Works at a party central office as adviser to party leaders. Former service in several ministries.

(6) *Economic journalist.* Former administrative class civil servant.

(7) *Economist.* Currently adviser to the head of a new administrative agency in national government. Former service in ministries.

(8) *Political scientist.* Specialist in public administration. Former Labour Parliamentary candidate.

(9) *Political scientist.* Teaches at a "new" university. Specialist in policy-making. Former Labour Parliamentary candidate.

(10) *Political scientist.* Teaches at a "new" university. Regular consultant to a ministry.

(11) *Political scientist.* Teaches at Oxford. Field is political and social theory.

(12) *Political scientist.* Former administrative class civil servant.

(13) *Political scientist.* Teaches at a "new" university.

(14) *Political scientist.* Active as a proponent of Parliamentary reform.

### B. Planners

(15) Works on long-range planning for London County Council.

(16) Is now teaching planning and doing research on the role of goals in planning after considerable planning experience.

(17) Director of a subregional planning study.

(18) Director of planning for a county council.

(19) Director of a regionwide planning study.

(20) Civil servant in Ministry of Housing and Local Government.

(21) Director of a program of rehabilitation of communities.

(22) Planner in the planning office of Liverpool.

(23) Economic planner for London County Council.

(24) Director of a subregional planning study.

## C. Lawyers

(25) *Barrister.* Former Conservative M.P. Active in Conservative Party bow group. Writer of pamphlets for the party on policy matters, seeks legal cases of "constitutional" import.

(26) *Barrister.* Former Labour Parliamentary candidate. Active as a lobbyist for race relations reform legislation. Graduate work in law in the United States and participation in the American civil rights movement.

(27) *Barrister.* Former Labour candidate. Active in race relations lobbying. Journalist on legal topics.

(28) *Barrister.* Recommended as an extremely skilled lawyer.

(29) *Barrister.* Specialized in planning law. Pleads both for government and private clients.

(30) *Barrister.* Conservative Parliamentary candidate. Active in the bow group.

(31) *Solicitor.* Active in the Law Society, the body which governs the solicitor's branch of the profession.

(32) *Solicitor.* Teaches law at a university. Active on a number of fronts in the reform of the legal profession. Studied and practiced law in the United States.

(33) *Solicitor.* Expert in planning law. Lobbies in both Parliamentary parties for improved planning law. Teaches for the Law Society.

(34) *Solicitor.* Active in the Law Society.

(35) *Solicitor.* In private practice with a firm which specializes in labor law. Also has a personal practice of race relations matters. Active as a lobbyist for race relations legislation. Taught and practiced law in the United States.

## D. Managers

(36) *Merchant banker* temporarily working in Whitehall department. Studied business administration in the United States.

(37) *Writer* on economic questions, currently serving as Whitehall administrator. Has worked in the United States.

(38) *Former financial analyst.* Now working in Whitehall as a temporary civil servant. Has worked in the United States.

(39) *Director* of the division of a large international corporation.

(40) *Director* of exports for a large international corporation.

(41) *Head* of a domestic division of a large corporation.

(42) *Director* of domestic sales for a large oil company.

(43) *Executive* of a company with extensive European sales.

(44) *Officer* of an international company. Former Conservative Parliamentary candidate.

(45) *Director* of research for a large corporation. Former civil servant.

(46) *Publisher.* National officer of a political party and former Parliamentary candidate.

# REFERENCES

ABEL-SMITH, B. and R. STEVENS (1967) Lawyers and the Courts: A Sociological Study of the English Legal System, 1790-1965. London: Heinemann.

ALTSHULER, A. (1965) The City Planning Process. Ithaca: Cornell Univ. Press.

BOORSTIN, D. (1968) The Americans: The Colonial Experience. New York: Random House.

CAVES, R. E. et al. (1968) Britain's Economic Prospects. Washington, D.C.: Brookings Institution.

CHANDLER, A. (1962) Strategy and Structure: Chapters in the History of the Industrial Enterprise. Cambridge, Mass.: MIT Press.

CHRISTOPH, J. (1965) "Consensus and cleavage in British political ideology." Amer. Pol. Sci. Rev. 59 (December).

The Civil Service (1968) Report of the Committee, 1966-1968. London: HMSO.

CRICK, B. [ed.] (1967) Essays on Reform. London: Oxford Univ. Press.

––– (1965) The Reform of Parliament. Garden City, N.Y.: Doubleday Anchor.

ECKSTEIN, H. (1962) "The British political system," in S. H. Beer and A. B. Ulam (eds.) Patterns of Government. New York: Random House.

FOLEY, D. (1963) Controlling London's Growth: Planning the Great Wen. Berkeley and Los Angeles: Univ. of California Press.

HAGE, G. and M. AIKEN (1971) Social Change in Complex Organizations. New York: Random House.

MACKINTOSH, J. P. (1971) "Specialist committees in the House of Commons: have they failed?" The Waverly Papers, Occasional Paper 1, Series 1, University of Edinburgh.

MITCHELL, W. C. (1967) Sociological Analysis and Politics: The Theories of Talcott Parsons. Englewood Cliffs, N.J.: Prentice-Hall.

PARKIN, F. (1968) Middle Class Radicalism. Manchester: Manchester Univ. Press.

PARSONS, T. (1968) "Professions," p. 12 in Volume 12 of D. Sills (ed.) International Encyclopedia of the Social Sciences. New York: Macmillan and Free Press.

PRICE, D. K. (1965) "The spectrum from truth to power," in The Scientific Estate. Cambridge, Mass.: The Belknap Press of Harvard University.

––– (1954) Government and Science. New York: New York Univ. Press.

PUSIC, E. (1969) "A theoretical model of the role of professionals in complex development situations," in G. Beneviste and W. Ilchman (eds.) Agents of Change: Professionals in Developing Countries. New York: Frederick A. Praeger.

RODWIN, L. (1956) The British New Towns Policy. Cambridge, Mass.: Harvard Univ. Press.

ROSE, R. (1965) "England: the traditionally modern political culture," in L. W. Pye and S. Verba (eds.) Political Culture and Political Development. Princeton: Princeton Univ. Press.

ROTHMAN, S. (1961) "Modernity and tradition in Britain." Social Research 28, 3.

Royal Commission on Local Government in England (1969). Short version of the Report on Local Government Reform. London: HMSO.

SAMPSON, A. (1962) The Anatomy of Britain. New York: Harper & Row.

SCHICK, A. (1971) "Toward the cybernetic state," in D. Waldo (ed.) Public Administration in a Time of Turbulence. San Francisco: Chandler.

THOMPSON, V. A. (1961) Modern Organization: A General Theory. New York: Alfred A. Knopf.

WALTZ, K. N. (1967) Foreign Policy and Democratic Politics. Boston: Little, Brown.

ERWIN C. HARGROVE *is professor and chairman of the Political Science Department at Brown University. He received his undergraduate and graduate degrees from Yale University and has been a member of the Brown faculty for twelve years. He is the author of* Presidential Leadership, Personality and Political Style *and is presently working on another study of the presidency. He has a number of articles on the subject of professionals in government which, along with the presidency and comparative study of leadership in the United States and England, is one of his major interests.*